May O'Donnell

Florida A&M University, Tallahassee
Florida Atlantic University, Boca Raton
Florida Gulf Coast University, Ft. Myers
Florida International University, Miami
Florida State University, Tallahassee
University of Central Florida, Orlando
University of Florida, Gainesville
University of North Florida, Jacksonville
University of South Florida, Tampa
University of West Florida, Pensacola

May O'Donnell

MODERN DANCE PIONEER

Marian Horosko

UNIVERSITY PRESS OF FLORIDA

Gainesville · Tallahassee · Tampa · Boca Raton · Pensacola · Orlando · Miami · Jacksonville · Ft. Myers

Copyright 2005 by Marian Horosko
Printed in the United States of America on acid-free paper
All rights reserved

10   09   08   07   06   05   6   5   4   3   2   1

p. viii. May O'Donnell in *Herodiade,* courtesy Isamu Noguchi
Museum.

All other photos courtesy O'Donnell/Green Foundation.

Library of Congress Cataloging-in-Publication Data
Horosko, Marian.
May O'Donnell: modern dance pioneer / Marian Horosko.
p. cm.
ISBN 0-8130-2857-4 (alk. paper)
1. O'Donnell, May, 1906-2004. 2. Dancers—United States—
Biography. 3. Choreographers—United States—Biography.
4. Modern dance. I. Title.
GV1785.042H67   2005
792.8'0929ab—dc22   2005048565

The University Press of Florida is the scholarly publishing agency
for the State University System of Florida, comprising Florida
A&M University, Florida Atlantic University, Florida Gulf Coast
University, Florida International University, Florida State
University, University of Central Florida, University of Florida,
University of North Florida, University of South Florida, and
University of West Florida.

University Press of Florida
15 Northwest 15th Street
Gainesville, FL 32611-2079
http://www.upf.com

Contents

Foreword

I never saw May O'Donnell perform live. I knew of her reputation as a leading dancer with Martha Graham and as an educator and a choreographer in her own right. I had heard of her lyricism as a dancer, and her quiet, powerful eloquence. I imagined that she must have been rather like the Pioneer Woman, seated and serenely gazing out past the horizon in Graham's *Appalachian Spring*, one of her most famous roles. She was one of those rare artists who could make stillness sing.

And then I got to meet May. I remember slogging along on shabby East Village streets, past motorcycle gangs and plump Hispanic "mamis" chatting intently on the sidewalk. This is where a famous dancer and choreographer lived? And then there was May, opening the door to my weary ring and advising me to tuck in, as I might in a dance class, because the door didn't open very wide. Inside was the most cozy of homes, complete with an amiable cat and an even more amiable husband, the composer Ray Green.

Here was a tall, slender woman with a delicately beautiful face who threw her head back and laughed like a longshoreman. The steel that helped her survive the Graham experience was evident, but even more evident was the dreamer who created her often mysterious dances and who reached for the depths in the greenest of her young dancers.

She told me the story, one day, of how she created her signature work, *Suspension*. And from that story I drew my image of May: a young woman whose mind and vision had been expanded by the open space and small-town California experiences of her childhood. Once, said, she saw a wartime plane fly by below her as she stood on a high hillside. Most of us simply would have been surprised for a moment by the sight of such a low-flying plane. But May sensed a reversal of expectation, the poetic readjustment of weight and space to be seen in suspended objects. There was dance, she knew, at T. S. Eliot's "still point of the turning world."

Jennifer Dunning, dance critic, New York Times

Preface

May O'Donnell: Modern Dance Pioneer is the first book on O'Donnell (1906–2004) as performer, choreographer, and teacher. She was hypnotizing on stage, a prolific choreographer, a distinguished teacher, and creator of her own technique and vocabulary. In conversations with the author over a two-year period, and using her collection of playbills and reviews, O'Donnell traced her journey of discovery from her early training in Sacramento, California; her first performance in 1928; study in New York at the Martha Graham School of Contemporary Dance; success in the Graham company; and the formation of her own choreographies and companies from 1937 to 1988.

O'Donnell instinctively knew that no matter how much she wanted to dance, classes in ballet at home and the form of modern dance she found in the Wigman studio in New York were not for her. She found her place in the Graham school, where Gertrude Shurr, a member of the company, taught, formed, and molded her strong body into a Graham dancer in record time. In 1932, O'Donnell joined the Graham company, performing from 1932 to 1938 in their repertory. But the mountains and sky, the fields and ocean of her native California lured her back. There she began work on her solo choreography (1937). She was immediately successful. O'Donnell established a school and company, married composer Ray Green, and co-choreographed and toured as a duo-concert team with José Limón from 1939 to 1941. The physical beauty of the two dancers, their prodigious technique, and their compelling presence caught fire. They got cheering reviews. World War II separated the team as Green and Limón went off to duty. Against the backdrop of the war, O'Donnell created her signature work, *Suspension* (1943). The hazardous conditions on the West Coast made her return to the Graham company from 1944 to 1954. Recognizing her choreographic ability and strong presence on stage, Graham gave her the privilege of choreographing her own roles. They were memorable: the Pioneer Woman in *Appalachian Spring* (1944), the Attendant in *Herodiade* (1944), *Dark Meadow* (1946), *Cave of the Heart* (1946), and other works.

After leaving the Graham company in 1954, she resumed her choreographic career and formed a studio and school with Gertrude Shurr. This highly active period brought a whirlwind of touring appearances with her companies, workshop engagements in the United States and London, teaching at the High School for the Performing Arts, and guest-teaching at summer intensives. Reviews were glowing. She and Green, who wrote most of her music, had worked together since 1937 and would continue to collaborate until 1988.

Yet the fame they deserved eluded them until they both were in their seventies, when the dance world suddenly awakened to their contributions to the legacy of modern dance. Always independent, they admitted that they didn't want a professional press person, patron, or manager to help them or "tell [them] what to do." The late recognition was lamentable, but it had permitted their interdependence to survive.

O'Donnell's house in Manhattan on East Seventh Street is now the center for the O'Donnell-Green Music and Dance Foundation. Ray's foresight in documenting their lives by collecting playbills, reviews, and photos lent this book much factual support. Duplicates are now being distributed to several dance collections in libraries in the United States and in Israel.

O'Donnell, until her death in a peaceful sleep on February 1, 2004, remained beautiful, meeting the assaults of aging with humor, serenity, and dignity intact. It was a privilege to have known her.

Thanks and acknowledgments go to all her family members, students, former company members, and friends, as well as to Rachel Yocum, former head of the Dance Division at the High School for the Performing Arts, who maintained contact with her over the years. Without the support and assistance of Roberto Garcia, acting executive director, and Frank Shawl, president of the O'Donnell-Green Foundation, this book would not have been possible. Journalists George Dorris and Jack Anderson charmed her and earned her admiration, as did Jennifer Dunning, dance critic at the *New York Times*. Neighbors Donna Farrimond and Mark Giammario were just down the street for her, as was Barbara Barr, who helped organize numerous boxes of memorabilia. Madeleine Nichols, curator of the Dance Division, New York Public

Library for the Performing Arts, Lincoln Center, gave us Patricia Raider to catalog material. Irene Morowski helped with photographs and videos. As always, editor Meredith Babb of the University Press of Florida answered all my questions with patience. And not least, thanks go to computer whiz Nicole Mizrachi, who could delve into my machine and come up with wonders.

The book serves as a reference for dance scholars and as an inspiration for dancers, teachers, and musicians, filling a missing link in dance history between the early pioneers and today's contemporary dance.

May O'Donnell

One January 2002

"There was this thing called modern dance," says May O'Donnell, "and everybody wanted to know about it, especially the gym teachers in the colleges."

May is now ninety-six years old with a clear memory and excellent health. She laughs easily and welcomes her frequent visitors—former students, dancers, friends. Her straight gray hair is cut short around her ears, and a twinkle remains in her dark blue eyes. Her high cheekbones have kept her face strong and beautiful. She is slender and uses her walker to slowly arrive at a chair near her dining room table, where we like to talk. Her back is straight. Her voice is strong and her speech pattern from the West Coast, where she was born. She answers questions directly, honestly, showing wisdom and unexpected humor. She is herself, the Pioneer Woman she created in Martha Graham's *Appalachian Spring*.

On December 2 of this year, May will receive a Martha Hill Lifetime Achievement Award. She looks forward more to honoring Martha Hill and Mary Jo Shelley—the founders of the Bennington College summer schools and festivals—than being honored herself.

The sun shines through the tall windows of her brownstone. The red brick house is on Seventh Street at Avenue C in Manhattan and dates from before the turn of the century. The small grand piano that belonged to her composer husband, Ray Green, remains silent now in the living room. Her garden, full of roses in the spring, small trees, and flowers, can be seen from her kitchen window. Next to her books are candleholders, a bowl, small items from her family's past. The furnishings throughout the house are simple.

Upstairs, on the second and third floors, her programs, photos, and letters are in boxes that date from the 1930s to the 1990s. They are being catalogued for the Dance Collection of the New York Public Library for the Performing

Arts at Lincoln Center and other libraries throughout the United States. Music scores, tapes, and videos are stored in the basement. "Ray," May says with a grin, "saved just everything!"

Pedro, her black-and-white cat, pads around the room. "We're the same age," she quips. "Come, Pedro, come." And the cat, trained to jump into her lap on the count of three, does a deep plié, jumps, lands, and begins to purr.

"It was in old houses like this one, with long living rooms and broad, planked wooden floors, where Martha [Graham], Charles [Weidman] and so many other early modern dancers taught class and gave performances.

"Martha's studio was at 66 Fifth Avenue in just such a building. We had daily technique classes, and Louis Horst taught us composition. Since I had music in my background in California, I took to his classes easily."

In 1934, at Bennington College and Undergraduate Liberal Arts College for Women, modern dance found its momentous exposure at the Bennington Summer Dance Festival. In 1932, before that historic summer when Doris Humphrey, Martha Graham, Charles Weidman, and Hanya Holm performed their techniques and vocabularies, May, Horst, and a small group of Graham dancers on tour explored the possibility of beginning classes at the college. Up to that point, modern dance had been more organized and developed in Europe, mainly under the influence of Mary Wigman (1886–1973), Germany's most famous modern dancer. Louis Horst and May, as his assistant, discovered that there was indeed a possibility for summers of dance at Bennington.

Mary Josephine Shelley was administrative director of student activity at the University of Chicago; Martha Hill, a member of the Graham company (1929–31), was head of the dance department at Bennington College. As founders, Shelley and Hill directed all the programs at the Bennington Summer Festival. In 1951, Hill also founded the dance division of the Juilliard School in Manhattan with the unheard of combination of ballet and modern dance teachers, notably Agnes de Mille, Martha Graham, Doris Humphrey, José Limón, Antony Tudor, Louis Horst, and Ann Hutchinson (dance notation).

"I can't imagine how long it would have taken for modern dance to expand without those two women, who provided a place to study, create, and rehearse and even a place to live and cafeteria service for those early artists, students, dance educators, and gym teachers who taught dance. And because so many of them came from universities, they began to book the modern dance choreographers that they had seen at Bennington. That created an audience, a small income for the companies and lots of exposure.

"Louis lorded over those poor teachers who came for the summer sessions," May remembers. "They were supposed to bring original dance pieces to class. He would tear each contribution down in front of the entire class. As his assistant, I would find them crying on my shoulder, and I had a devil of a time getting them to calm down. 'Don't pay any attention to Louis on that score,' I'd say; 'he does that to everybody!'

"But outside of class, they were nice to me and Louis. They had paying jobs, cars, and money to spend, and they would take us out to dinner. Of course, they wanted Louis to like their compositions and wanted to pamper him. If something looked strange, he would say 'strange is beautiful.' At the end of the summer, there would be a little group demonstration of their work. That pleased them."

Martha's contraction-and-release principle is still in May's body. She demonstrates the principle while sitting in her chair. "I always think of the release as a lift," she explains. "I love the feel of it. It's almost as if I'm going to take off. Every movement you do in dance has to be alive like that."

Two California, 1920s, Early Lessons

May was born in Sacramento, California, on May 1, 1906, to Ada Augusta Herbert and James O'Donnell. She was christened Marie Daphne, but her brothers called her May because she was born on the first day of that month. Her mother had been raised by an aunt and uncle from Australia who loved the outdoors.

May was shy her entire life and found herself always in the back row of a group her own age because she was taller. Eventually she learned to use her height to her advantage.

May's mother and her brother, Horace Herbert, loved music but had had no opportunity for formal study. Horace began the musical training for the O'Donnell children with trumpet lessons for May's older brother, Bill.

"I remember," says May, "being taken to a symphony concert in San Francisco. It was the first time I ever saw or heard an orchestra. We sat in the gallery. The shock of sound was electric. It made my spine tingle. I couldn't believe the sensation. I also remember seeing Pavlova dance [1924 in Oakland] and heard Paderewski play."

When May returned from San Francisco, she asked her father for piano lessons, and he bought her a piano. He took great pride in the musical ability of his children. "I studied piano," May remembers, "with Sister Philomena at the St. Francis Parochial School in Sacramento, where I was enrolled in 1912 and later studied with Albert Elkus, a well-known pianist and composer in Sacramento, San Francisco, and the Bay Area.

"I had three brothers—Bill, who played the trumpet in a band, and after I was born, there was Herb and Charlie. We remained in touch throughout our lives.

"My grandparents had homesteaded the land. The family was Catholic, and confession became a trial for me. I couldn't think of anything to confess, so I used to make up things. Later, my family went each an individual way in the choice of religion.

"I played 'statues' with my girlfriends outdoors every Saturday. We did something called 'snap the whip' where we'd hang on to each other's arms and run in a circle until I yelled 'stop.' The prettiest pose would be the winner. Everyone had to be in a statue pose of a notable or a typical profession. My first choreography was praise for whatever appeared to be a recognizable statue.

"My father worked for the Southern Pacific, so we traveled everywhere on passes. I was deeply impressed with the beauty of the land, its colors, lines, and contours. There were so many trees, vineyards, birds, and animals, and I loved the view of the Sierra Nevada Mountains in the distance. I think those elements became movement and line in my work at a later date.

"I saw a dance recital by students of Leila Maple and was taken with it, seeing those girls with their curls. I think the teacher might have been in some Denishawn summer courses. Years later, when I told Gertrude Shurr, who had been in the Denishawn company, she thought so as well. I wanted to study dance but was tall for my age and strong and didn't seem the type for ballet. Playing games with my brothers made me feel like one of them.

"There was little money available with all the music lessons in the family, and since I loved to practice the piano, there was no giving that up for dance lessons. I saw a dance recital when I was in high school. It was the most beautiful, the most wondrous thing I had ever seen. Dancing is what I wanted to do. Playing the piano in public was terrifying, but dancing seemed natural. I worked hard at the piano and qualified to study with Elkus.

"A student of Maple said to me that if we could get four people together, we could have a dance class that would cost only a dollar each. I roped in a cousin of mine and a friend's cousin to make our foursome. Since I wanted to dance so badly, my mother encouraged me and bought me a pair of ballet slippers and a little chiffon skirt. I found myself at fourteen years of age, the tallest, again, and the oldest girl in the class. But the teachers liked me because I did everything I was told to do and because I encouraged the class to practice. It got to the point where I made everyone practice high kicks, or they weren't my friend anymore. I was a little embarrassed being so tall and older, but I stuck it out and was in one of Maple's recitals. I played for classes [1923–24] in exchange for dance lessons. I studied ballet for about three years and was in the studio morning, noon, and night. I had found my life.

"It was difficult for parents of young students who had to travel far along the levy, where the Sacramento River was about to wander into the San Francisco Bay, to get to class. To make it easier for them, Maple's teachers asked me to teach a weekly session in a small space that was part of the local post office. We used a record player for accompaniment. My mother and I would pile into the car every Saturday with our dog, 'Blackie,' hanging out of the window and Herb driving us to my class. I taught in more than one little town. It all lasted for a couple of years.

"My mother was so open and encouraging it was a blessing. I was given tremendous freedom. I was graduated from high school and started junior college until I realized that I could not become a dancer by going to college. I did a half year of French, English, and two courses that looked interesting—eurhythmics and harmony, which were about rhythm exercises. I represented my school in a San Francisco fair by composing a piano piece called 'Rain.'

"But I knew that I would never be a ballet dancer, so I tried acrobatics taught by an old hoofer in San Francisco, where I went on my father's railroad pass. I was terrified by it. A girl in the Maple studio told me of the Estelle Reed Studio in San Francisco. It was time to make a change.

"As I went down the stairs to the Reed studio on Geary Street and looked in, I saw a class in progress. I asked, 'Is this what you call modern dance?' Mrs. Reed answered, 'Come on in, honey," and there I was. It was Estelle's mother who manned the desk and told me that Estelle was in Europe studying at the Wigman school. Estelle was a free soul and typical of a jazz age rebel. She was too big physically to be a ballet person, just as I wasn't built for it either. Mrs. Reed let me stay with her because I couldn't go back and forth to Sacramento. I lived in her apartment, helped with errands and with the studio. I played piano for some classes in exchange for dance classes. Reed's teachers taught some of the work Estelle had been taught in Germany. It felt right for me.

"Finally, Estelle returned from Europe. She was sophisticated and had a special quality about her. Her ballet training had been with former Diaghilev Ballet Russe dancer Theodore Koslov, in Los Angeles, but somewhere along the line, she got caught up in what was going on in Europe. She knew about

1. One-year-old May, Sacramento, 1907.

2. May at nine years, 1915.

3. May in 1918.

Laban and Dalcroze, as well as Wigman, and was doing some choreography on her own. We did a little program with her in San Francisco. She chose five of us, Betty Noyes, La Viva del Curo, Bernice Cameron (because she looked like Isadora), Eva May Butts (who omitted her last name for stage), and me for a trip to Europe.

"Reed got us together as a little company for the tour. Off I went with one of the girls on my father's pass to New York, where the tour would begin, with a big basket lunch and a basket of fruit. The trip was exciting and a big adventure. My mother and father saw us off. In New York, we boarded a French boat."

In the middle of the Atlantic, one of the worst storms of the century got the boat rolling on the high seas. Not knowing that they should be scared, they thought it was fun.

4. The Estelle Reed group sets sail: Bernice Cameron, May O'Donnell, Estelle Reed, La Viva del Curo, Eva May Butler, Betty Noyes, New York, 1928.

Tél.: Elysées 79-46   BUREAU de CONCERTS MARCEL de VALMALÈTE. 45, Rue La Boëtie. Paris-8°   R. C. Seine 311-047

COMÉDIE DES CHAMPS-ELYSÉES
13-15, Avenue Montaigne

SAMEDI 25 OCTOBRE 1930 à 16 heures
(Ouverture des portes à 15 h. 30)

MATINÉE DE DANSE

ESTELLE
REED

et son Groupe de Danseuses
(STUDIO ESTELLE REED DE SAN-FRANCISCO, CALIFORNIE)

**Betty NOYES, Eva MAY, May O' DONNELL,
Bernice CAMERON, La VIVA del CURO.**

AU PIANO : WOLFGANG WYDEVELD

PROGRAMME AU VERSO

5. Estelle Reed program, 1928.

"It was 1928, and I was twenty-two and had five hundred dollars for the trip. I was so excited. We arrived in Paris where Estelle gave us warnings, because we were so unsophisticated, about how innocent we were and how seductive European men could be. We got so we didn't dare look at anyone. We were like nuns and always a little nervous. We were in Paris over the Christmas holidays.

"In Paris, we stayed at a small pension near the American University at St. Michaels. If we missed a pension meal, we missed eating. Ballet classes were taught by La Viva because Estelle didn't seem interested in teaching us any longer, but she wanted our utter devotion. We visited the museums and went to Montparnasse. What an awakening! We were all eyes. We saw movies of Bali and Vietnam. And we saw the masters of Dutch painting as well as modern artists.

"We left very soon for Holland for the engagements Estelle had arranged. There was only one concert in Utrecht, a few nightclub dates, and nothing more because of poor organization. We gave that performance in Holland because Estelle had married there and wanted to start the tour in Utrecht. She eventually settled in Curacao, where her husband had been sent by the Dutch government to be council general. We did a concert in Amsterdam, The Hague, and one in Paris. In Utrecht, we lived in a pension on a canal, but bathing was a problem. The first of the week, you had to wash your hair, your body, and your clothes, which cost extra. The Depression was worldwide, and we had to write home for more money.

"We found a little studio in Utrecht, and La Viva and Betty Noyes, who had studied with Mary Ann Wells in Seattle, gave us ballet class. We were disappointed that Estelle did not teach.

"Estelle's choreography was not great. She did the solos, and we were the surrounding group. After a spring and winter, there were no further concerts. We had seen a lot of Europe but were ready to go back to America. I regretted the loss of classes during the tour and later said so to Reed. She agreed. But the performing and touring experience were invaluable.

"After that long, cold winter, we went to the North Sea for some engagements in a big movie house. It was hardly on the level of Denishawn. We were the intermission entertainment on an open floor in the salon. The audience had tea, something to eat, and was entertained by jugglers, comedians, and other acts. Our costume consisted of turkey feathers sewed on a headband, shorts, a bra, and Wigman slippers. We were not reengaged.

"Late in 1930, we did a concert in Paris. Estelle told us we had to find our way back to the States on our own. Three of us went home directly, but I stayed with one of the girls. We had met two musicians who we liked very much. I wanted to see a lot more while waiting for the next boat. The two musicians, a Dutch boy, and the other, who was Spanish, knew what was going on in Paris, so it was intellectually stimulating. Finally, we booked onto an English freighter stopping in Rotterdam, London, the Caribbean, South and Central America. I ate more bananas on that trip than Tarzan's little monkey 'Cheetah'!

"In the summer of 1931, by brother Bill took a course at the University of California in Los Angeles for his music degree. I shared his house and decided to take a course with Michio Ito [Japanese dancer and choreographer, 1892–1961]. Pauline Koner was in his company, and I had seen a performance in San Francisco. Ito traveled around the country teaching his technique, which included a great deal of footwork and his famous ten arm gestures. He demanded that the center of the body, the core, be held securely, which was probably from training learned during his expressionist European background. Estelle, who was fascinating as a performer, had used some of his little preludes, but they didn't impress me. The movements were too small and delicate for me. But it was there that someone suggested I go to New York to study with Martha Graham.

"We did one last performance for Estelle that was at the Geary Theater in San Francisco, April 12, 1931. Although I resented her not giving us more classes on the tour to improve our technique, the experience of the trip to Europe had taught me a great many things.

"My father had died in a railroad accident in 1931, but we still could use his train passes. My mother and I took the train up to the Canadian Pacific railroad. We packed our own provisions for the long journey, which was like a pioneering experience. The trains had pot-bellied stoves for people to cook their own meals on board. We crossed from the West Coast to the East Coast on that train.

"We continued on to New York, where it was winter and freezing. The Depression had made money scarce for everyone, but I had to keep searching for the right place for me. My mother returned to California, and I stayed and shared a room at the YMCA. It was time to continue to find my place in this thing called 'modern dance.'"

Three Study in New York, 1930s

May is anxious to talk about her early training in New York. She nibbles on a Graham cracker, takes a sip of tea, and begins. "Come, Pedro," she says to her cat, "one-two-three."

"Wigman had a studio in New York at Steinway Hall on Fifty-seventh Street. Carnegie Hall was across the street, and all the big agents had offices up and down the street. I had seen Wigman [1886–1973] perform in San Francisco in 1930. She impressed me as being powerful, Germanic, and down-to-earth."

The Wigman school had flourished in Dresden, but the Nazi government had little sympathy for an art they considered decadent, and Wigman's appearance at the Berlin Olympic games in 1935 was one of her last. The Nazis closed the school, and she went elsewhere.

"The Wigman school in New York seemed well organized, so I took some classes with Fé Ahlff but stopped because Wigman wasn't there much of the time. The studio in Steinway Hall was run by Hanya Holm and managed by the famous impresario Sol Hurok. Ahlff was a big German girl and quite beautiful. Her class consisted of no exercises on the floor, no warm-up, just patterns that we were to imitate as we tagged behind her across the floor to the sound of a drum. The classes began with a walk—a little walk with a side step—and then became more complicated. I had no idea what I was doing. Ahlff never turned around to see what the class was doing. It was heady, but I wasn't learning anything. A student, Jerome Andrews, took me under his wing and said: 'Look, Mary Wigman is coming here on a tour, and she's interested in improvisation.' So I got invited to the class where Wigman was going to observe improvisation. It was a word I didn't know. It turned out to be a class where we were all spread out on the floor and were supposed to be rocks.

Jerome said: 'Just follow me, May.' We were told that we were to be *nothing* and had to become *something*. It was chaotic. Jerome was so uninhibited, I was embarrassed. His reaction to the class was to go to Paris. Mine was to go to Martha Graham.

"In 1932, the Graham school was on Ninth Street, between University Place and Broadway. The classes were in the long, narrow parlor of a small brownstone building. And there I sat between Jane Dudley and Sophie Maslow. Martha taught class sitting on the floor with us. It consisted of stretches and lifts, something easy for me to do. There seemed to be a progressive technique, and that was just what I wanted. Everything felt good. I was naturally strong and very disciplined. The classes were so crowded that there was no room to move anywhere but in your own space. There was a lot of work in opposition, which is one part of the body working against another part. The contraction-and-release principle was taught. There were back falls, long stretches in the thighs that took strength, and brushes.

"The social and artistic attitude at the time was: return to the primitive. Down with anything decorative. Ballet was in a poor state at the time. The entire art world, music, and dance began searching for new ways to express itself.

"Compared to the Wigman school, the Graham atmosphere seemed more personal. One day in class, Martha called me aside and said: 'If you learn some of my things and work with one of my people, I think I might use you in some of my dances.' I was big and strong. Most of her girls were small. Coming from the West, my movements were more open, and I think Martha liked that contrast.

"The prospect was frightening and wonderful. One of her teachers was Gertrude Shurr, who had come from Denishawn. Gertrude loved Martha, and that's all she had to hear. If Martha had asked her to teach a frog, Gertrude would have taught one. She had taken over the summer course in 1930, while Martha and Louis Horst took a trip to Indian country near Santa Fe for research. I worked hard for Gert, who turned me inside out and became a lifelong friend, as well as a colleague. At that time, I was bashful. Now I can't stop talking!

"Martha lived in the back of the house on Ninth Street. She seemed very serious and evidently liked my energy and willingness to work hard. She didn't sympathize with her students. I had learned my lesson to keep a distance between us because of my disappointment in Estelle Reed. That lesson served me well in my entire relationship over the years with Martha.

"When the school moved to 66 Fifth Avenue, the larger space permitted us to move across the floor in low walks, run in place, and to take long strides with many variations in counts and direction. Prances were added, and triplets as well as running steps. I went to live in Gertrude's place on Eleventh Street, where Lillian Shapiro and several other dancers lived.

"At that time, life wasn't easy for any modern dancer, nor was it for Martha until she was awarded a Guggenheim grant. Political liberals were interested in modern dance only as part of the social change going on in the thirties. Because ballet wasn't very good in this country at that time, it was no wonder that it was rejected to some extent. Gertrude and I went to ballet performances because we wanted to see everything. But modern dance was our dance, American, not from another culture. Our freedom gave us the right to discover and explore. No government sponsorship could dictate to us. Of course, we had to pay our own way. But we managed.

"The West Coast was just as anxious as the East to find a new form. The West had always been adventurous and free from convention. So we did just that. We experimented and found our own way. The arts were helping each other to find new paths. Painting, music, and politics—all were searching and rejecting the past. I was appalled at the passionate feelings of some of our group for communism and social reform. There was yelling in the streets along with the parades. You can imagine how scary it was for a simple girl from Sacramento, even when I boarded a bus. I didn't care about politics. I only wanted to dance."

And dance she did until her last performance in 1961.

Four Louis Horst and Early Days at Bennington

"Louis Horst never got as much credit as he deserved," began May. Horst (1884–1964), a Kansas City–born pianist, was the composer of Martha Graham's *Primitive Mysteries* (1931), *Ceremonials* (1932), *Frontier* (1935), *El Penitente* (1940), and many more smaller works.

"He knew Martha from her Denishawn days, when he had been the group's musical director [1915–25]. He had toured with Martha in that company, and when she went on her own, he became her mentor. When she produced her first recital in 1926, Louis (pronounced Lou-ee) was her accompanist at the piano. There was a personal relationship between them. Horst had become interested in modern music and expressionism when he had studied composition in Vienna. And Martha, with her searching desire for new movement, was comfortable with his new discoveries.

"Louis believed in structure, discipline, and control, which I appreciated because of my early musical background. He made you bring movement to him. A piece in some kind of form. He wanted a core in a movement that was devoid of decoration, and he was blunt about it. He would sit there and look stabbed in the back if you didn't follow his way! But I stuck it out because dance composition was what I wanted to do most."

After World War I, the entire art world, in an effort to return to basics, sought primitive art as a new beginning point. African sculpture and the work of Picasso and Henry Moore were discovered. Martha was motivated by the culture of our Southwest Indians and became inspired to create *Primitive Mysteries, El Penitente, Frontier,* and *Ceremonials.*

"She wanted to keep Louis busy, needed, and nearby," May continued. "He selected all her music and gave good advice. He was a strong influence in many ways. At one point, Martha felt that her girls would benefit from more knowledge of music. We were to do little dances, and Louis would accompany the pieces. He was tough, sarcastic, and would yell at us enough to make all of us shake. I loved the classes. Louis would play a little composition and hope that the girls would remember the rhythm when they came to the next class. They were supposed to build a dance on that time signature. It was difficult for some of them, so I offered to help, if they would come to the little place Gert and I shared. I would play the work over and over on the piano until they sort of got it.

"Louis, at one point, wanted us to do something different. An archaic study. I was fascinated by a Greek statue in the Metropolitan Museum, especially one that seemed to be a young man walking. It seemed to be lifting off the floor. So my dance was about standing still, just concentrating and walking in place. I thought he would start to yell, but he didn't.

"He called Martha over to see it, and I performed it every time we demonstrated our little pieces. Louis wanted you to understand that a pavane was different from an allemande. He used *Orchésographie* by Thoinot Arbeau [1519–96] as our textbook to his course on preclassic dance forms. Louis wanted us to experience the rhythms of a period because he thought it reflected the people in their time. He didn't want us to use ballet steps nor rely too much on the music. That could have been a reaction to the music visualization performed by Denishawn. He and Martha felt that you could take the counts for a piece and add the music later. Martha worked this way many times. Louis's criticism was constructive. He liked the fact that I kept discarding, discarding, and discarding until I was satisfied. Many of the girls were frightened to death of him, and some would not come back to the class. I stayed in his class for eight years!

"We experienced the music and created a movement that revealed its structure. When Anna [Sokolow] did an allemande, she wasn't expressing herself, but the movement that fit the music in time and space. When Sophie [Maslow] did a pavane, it was honest to the structure of the music, but her own movement. I got assigned a gigue that I later enlarged as *Gigue for a Concert* [1934] for Robert Joffrey and Gerald Arpino when they were in one of my companies.

"At one point, Martha put all our little pieces together, and we performed them at colleges. Teachers who had come to our classes invited us to perform

6. Gertrude Shurr, Louis Horst, and May O'Donnell at Bennington, 1932.

in their schools. We also did performances in the studio. That gave us the performance opportunities we needed. With the music courses, Louis felt important, and Martha had found a way to keep him busy and involved in her company. He was a sensitive rehearsal taskmaster who didn't miss a thing. He kept us rehearsing well into the small hours of the night until everyone did everything correctly, and he would stand backstage in the wings during every performance. Woe to anyone who missed a beat or gave a flabby performance. All in all, it was a good period for growth and education for all of us.

"Louis was attracted to the girls, but we all knew that he and Martha were a pair. There was nothing to do in the summer evenings at Bennington College except sit and look at the moon. At one point, when Louis was sitting next to me, I found his wandering fingers running down my ankle. I quietly removed his hand, and nothing was said at that or any other time. Once I discovered that Louis wouldn't bother me after I gave him that slight rebuke, there were no hard feelings between us.

"I was at the Bennington Summer School of Dance from 1932, as Louis's assistant the first year, when our goal was to determine if a modern dance summer school and festival was possible. After that, I was Martha's assistant through 1938, except for 1937, when Gert and I were sent by Martha to teach in San Francisco at Betty Horst's school. Betty Horst was married to Louis in some kind of amiable relationship. They were never divorced.

"Martha, Charles [Weidman], Hanya [Holm], and Doris [Humphrey] did big pieces at Bennington and taught their techniques beginning in 1934. It was wonderful. It turned the tide for American dance from Europe, where dancers and teachers had to go to study new movements. We were discouraged from peeking at someone else's rehearsal. There was a sense of having a cause, of being able to reflect the times and express what could not be expressed otherwise.

"The summer school had rules, and although Mary Jo Shelley and Martha Hill, who put the school and festivals together, tried to keep the atmosphere calm, there was constant pressure. Martha was tense because of time constraints to produce.

"But modern dance had found a home, a base, and it wasn't in Europe, and it began to grow fast.

"The group watched over me as a church. There was a lot going on in New York in the early 1930s. There was constant unrest, deprivation, and endless protests. New York was nervous. People were struggling everywhere because of the Depression; the crash had been worldwide. We, too, struggled for a definition of what we were doing. Several of Martha's girls were Communists and were always rushing out to be in parades. It was their form of protest. There were lots of liberals in our audiences, and there was a lot of odd stuff going on all over the world, yelling and excited screaming. I never gave a damn about it. I had to just leave it be. I learned to keep my mouth shut. But it made me feel alone and not part of all the activity outside the studio. If I had not had Gertrude's friendship, I don't think I would have stuck it out. Gertrude, who was a born New Yorker, kept saying not to pay attention to this or that. She was so level-headed.

"Since my father had died in a railroad accident, and there was no money coming from home, I had to earn money by modeling for the rich ladies who took up painting or sculpting. I played the piano for classes here and there as well. Money was hard to come by, but I managed. Martha wanted me, and that's all Gertrude had to know. She made me work so that I'd be right for Martha. When we ran out of money or food, we'd go up to Gertrude's family in the Bronx and come back with enough food for a week. Gert's Jewish family accepted me because they thought I was a good, straightforward character and would keep Gertrude out of trouble. Little did they know that it was the other way around!"

May got some jobs. One offer to teach in Washington, D.C., at the August King Smith School for Girls came as a result of a demonstration given by May, Dorothy Bird, and Bonnie Bird. Martha gave the job to May. She went to Washington each week to give two classes on Monday afternoons, another on Tuesdays. It practically paid for her living expenses. She made the trip for two or three years. May also taught at the Fifty-third Street "Y" twice a week. Most dancers at the time, as they do now, took extra jobs to continue their study or to see them through nonpaying rehearsal periods.

"There was little financial support even for performances," May adds, "except for a gift from someone every now and again. In those days, it put a lot of pressure on the results of a New York opening. Although Martha had a following, there was always anxiety to create the next successful work. She'd rant and rave, convinced that all would be a failure. But all became a success.

"Some of the girls behaved badly, crying and acting out of control on opening nights. I thought of an opening as if it were a test in crossing the Rockies. Either you made it, or you didn't. I told the girls that they should get out of the group or stop complaining. I never forgot my experience with Estelle Reed, so I kept my distance from Martha. I kept my mouth shut, worked hard, and benefited from it.

"Martha was a force that was exciting and at the same time, violent. She wanted people who could be aggressive because it would show in their performance. She wanted emotions to show. In the early days, when there was hardly any money, she would sit on the floor thinking, and we'd stand around waiting for a long time. Things would begin to unfold as we rehearsed.

"Creating little dances for Louis to evaluate continued as part of everyone's training. I guess you could call those experiments our first choreographic attempts. They paved the way for us to be future creators. He was constantly demanding and never satisfied with ordinary solutions. His mission was to make us explore, search, and dare to do something not done before.

7. May soaring at Bennington, 1933.

"At Bennington, there were two different camps of people: the professional dancers who were poor, and the people in education who had the where-withal. People in education and professional dancers still split into two camps even today. But then it was worse. When they were on the floor working, they revealed themselves as kind of pathetic. They might become good teachers, and that wouldn't take anything away from them, but I felt sorry for them because they couldn't lift a leg, since they had no reason to. They were really volleyball players. I made it as easy for them as I could, and I certainly was sympathetic. But overall, there was a separation. They did the most marvelous thing for American dance. They got it on the map. They got the tours and residencies going, and eventually they themselves got better.

"But Louis, on the other hand, because he worked in his composition classes with people who were not basically dancers, and who had to teach dance at home because it was starting to come up, was encouraging. They had not had time to catch up. They were trying to get information and material to teach. He helped them and was shrewd enough to know that they were the people who were going to support dance in America and spread the word.

"On occasion, I would go West to visit my family, and once Gert went with me. We got onto what seemed to be a sort of freighter that went around the Panama Canal to San Francisco. It was fun, and we made friends with everyone on the boat. Coming back, we took a bus and visited Martha and Louis in Santa Fe, where Martha's Americana period had begun with Southwest Indian rituals.

"Although Louis and Martha loved one another, they didn't live together. Louis loved teaching and encouraging the talent in Martha's group, as well as helping with Martha's career."

In 1933, Horst established a publication, *Dance Observer,* that gave impetus to local dance criticism. He, along with John Martin and Walter Terry, were the first prominent critics who won support for modern dance.

By 1933, May had earned enough money from a few jobs to pay her share for a large studio on East Ninth Street with Gertrude Shurr. It was not far from Martha's, and they shared space with a Swedish masseuse. They had a ground floor with an old piano. They let Horst use it for his composition classes. He also taught at the Neighborhood Playhouse, a school for actors that included, and still does, Graham technique in the curriculum.

"Louis got good work from some of the dancers," May remembered, "especially from Anna and Sophie. Martha backed up Louis by insisting that we had to put something together for the classes. She scared us and often argued with Louis about movements in one of her works. But when all was settled, he was a marvelous rehearsal person as well, especially for *Primitive Mysteries,* where everything had to be dead right. And it was.

"The second year at Bennington [1935], Martha created *Panorama* at the end of the season. John Martin gave lectures on dance history, and we rehearsed until eleven o'clock at night. We were exhausted."

Five Success in the Graham Company

"Martha kept her promise that if I worked hard, she would put me into her dances. I joined her company in 1932 and stayed until 1938. The technique at that time was contained and required concentration. There wasn't much movement as a pattern. The new works in 1932 were *Ceremonials* and *Chorus of Youth-Companions,* along with four or five new works that didn't last in the repertory and others from earlier times. *Chorus* was a work Martha didn't demonstrate for us at rehearsals. She would try to get us to move a certain way, beginning, for instance, with our running in a circle, then changing the tempo of the run, or adding a fall or a jump. I was understudy in several works and then performed them. My first ballet was in *Primitive Mysteries* [1931], and it turned out to be my baptism by fire because it was so formal, so stylized.

"There was no pay for rehearsals, and we worked almost every day and almost every night. We were happy to receive five or ten dollars at the end of the concert year."

Colleges had begun to offer opportunities for modern dance performances, and there was a great deal of travel within the United States. Dancers in the Graham company, from 1930 to 1939, in addition to May and Gertrude, were Anita Alvarez, Thelma Babitz, Bonnie Bird, Dorothy Bird, Sydney Brenner, Ethel Butler, Grace Cornell, Merce Cunningham, Jane Dudley, Jean Erdman, Nelle Fisher, Frieda Flier, Nina Fonaroff, Beatrice Gerson, Ailes Gilmore (designer Isamu Noguchi's sister), Georgia Graham (Martha's sister), Mattie Haim, Elizabeth Halpern, Natalie Harris, Erick Hawkins, Martha Hill, Lil Liandre, Marie Marchowsky, Sophie Maslow, Lily Mehlman, Freema Nadler, Pauline Nelson, Mary Raoin, Florence Schneider, Bessie Schönberg, Catherine Selby, Kathleen Slanle, Anna Sokolow, Housely Stevens Jr., Martha Todd, Mildred Wile, and Joan Woodruff.

"Martha was getting better known and had support from the teachers who went to the Bennington summer study. We had tours booked in places like Nebraska and some concerts in schools where the teachers ran physical education departments. We traveled by train and shared everything, as did Martha. It was a question of who could get to the bathroom first to take care of basic necessities. There was no privacy.

"Everyone, everywhere, was amazed that we didn't wear shoes. The stages were so bad, it was a wonder our feet were not all cut up. Our costumes were long, flowing gowns in various colors. Louis, we assumed, booked the dates, but we didn't know for sure and never thought to ask. We got so little money, no weekly pay or union scale, that I don't even remember anyone giving me payment. But we had what we needed.

"We had a little three-piece orchestra that provided accompaniment, then later a larger group with clarinet, oboe, piccolo, drums, and piano and two male musicians with Louis as pianist and leader. We usually opened the program with *Celebration* [1934]. It was a dance in which we never stopped jumping, and the audience loved it.

"I remember once we were booked in Wyoming in a boys' college. There was lots of excitement until the boys saw us perform. We looked physically stronger than their football team!

"On one tour, a wealthy woman in the South put us up. There was a pool and we could swim, dive, and take a bath. It was heaven.

"As time went on, Martha gave me little parts to do that embarrassed me. I was sure it made the other girls angry. The girls were young and ambitious and had made so many sacrifices to stay with the group. They were competitive and given to histrionics and had what today we call 'an attitude.' But because I was tall and very strong, there were parts for that. The other girls were flexible and could move around fast. I was always in the back line. I felt like a toadstool, always there. But at times I was a balance and support for Martha in contrast to her small stature in roles that needed my quietness.

"I remember a role Martha gave me that had me standing center stage, looking upwards as I seemed to walk in place, while the girls ran around in a frenzy of fear. It wasn't until years later that I learned the work was Martha's response to the Spanish Civil War and that I was looking at bombs raining down. It was a section called *Steps in the Street* from *Chronicle* [1936]. Martha

8. May (*with leg up*) in Graham's *Celebration*, 1934.

9. May (*fifth from left*) in Graham's *Course*, 1935.

10. May, in "Hill Song" section of Graham's *Horizons,* 1936.

11. May, rehearsing in her San Francisco studio, 1937.

12. May in "Hail" from her *What So Proudly We Hail,* 1937.

never made explanations. We had to find our own inner meanings. Martha would, however, use images for class movements, but there was no explanation of what anything meant for stage. The movement for me in this work, or lack of it, was in placing one foot before the other, as if walking, but I never moved from the spot as the other dancers ran around me in terror. Maybe Martha remembered my Greek piece. Now that I think of it, I should have gotten ten dollars more for each performance! Martha also gave small solos to Anna Sokolow, Dorothy Bird, and Sophie Maslow.

"There was one piece in which I was, again, in the center doing a slow hinge backwards while everyone was dancing around me. It was torture. Martha liked a contrast of one slow movement against swift group movements. I got credit on the program for it. Martha was always generous in giving credit to her dancers. Because my knee-to-hip bone is long, it permitted me to arch

13. May in "Cornerstone" section from her first work of eighteen solos, *What So Proudly We Hail*, 1937.

backwards from a standing or kneeling position and to hold my balance with the support of a strong back.

"I saw that Martha could hurt with words, and since I had decided before I got into the company that it was better not to be too close to her, I escaped most of the hurt. She did no mentoring and kept a friendly distance. In looking back, maybe I was afraid of her and didn't want to be put into the position of being in her path. We had a conversation once in which she said that I was too mysterious for her. I said that I loved working for her and that I loved her, but that I remembered things got kind of crazy once in a while during rehearsals when she would yell at people. She didn't have the decency to tell someone in private that she was displeased but preferred to make it all into a dramatic event. I simply said that I could work with her better if I was not too close. It became a good and enduring relationship.

14. Composer
Ray Green, San
Francisco, 1937.

"I had danced in *Heretic* [1929], which was very formal and almost a ritual. I found it good for me so that I wouldn't be too open in my movements which were more natural to me. It made me realize, again, that following Martha was the right choice for me rather than following Doris Humphrey, who I admired but was more lyrical. There were other works that were solely movement pieces, but they didn't last in the repertory.

"Martha always did her solo *Lamentation* [1930] with great success. *Primitive Mysteries* played as if the audience were spying on a secret.

"The girls at that time had different bodies from the girls who do the dances now. They were more stolid and less flexible. The ones who lasted were the ones who could adjust to Martha's new movements as she adjusted to them. There were always changes in the technique over time. Martha never fixed any exercise but was constantly making changes. Later, there were many disputes over the correct way to do an exercise.

"In *Panorama,* her work got more lyrical. Martha created *Horizon Song* [1936] and then *American Document* [1938]. It was a work in several sections depicting the growth of the country. Martha was broadening her Americana period. The work was literal with several sections: Indian, Puritan, Emancipation, and Declaration. It was the first time Martha used a male dancer, Erick Hawkins, which led to new directions and challenges.

"Ray Green wrote the music for *American Document* after I showed Louis the score that Ray had written for my first large choreographic piece, *Of Pioneer Women* [1937], in San Francisco. It was for the summer school presentation at Bennington. That work led to another American work by Martha, *Letter to the World* [1940].

"As the number of dances increased, the movement enlarged and became even more demanding. There were signposts in the works over the years showing her growth and range. Of course, when you are in a work, you only see rehearsals, usually without Martha, who you saw only from the wings. Afterwards, when you saw the whole thing from the audience, you could see the transitions from her Denishaw-like solos, to protest works, political statements, pure movement pieces, Americana, and then the myths. But at the time, no one, probably not even Martha, knew where she was going except to make her feelings concrete. Many pieces fell by the wayside only to return in another form in another work at a later time.

"That period from 1932 to 1938 was a time to which I knew I would never return. I was a devoted student who wanted to be the very best. I warmed-up before rehearsal in order to get into the rehearsal immediately. It was all like being an apprentice in a religious order, and I kept myself in a kind of pure state without any extraneous distractions, such as looking at shops or beautiful clothes. I had no need for that. Of course it was hard because of my own frustrations and Martha's. But I never questioned what she did or judged it because it was absolutely right for her. As long as I was with her, I knew that her overall intentions were faultless and that her goal was my goal as well. I believed in modern dance. If we had no art, there wasn't much left except a world of money. I vaguely felt that the day would come when I would like to explore the world of movement within myself, but as long as I was with her, I didn't think too much about it.

"After I left the company in 1938 to do my own work in California, Martha would call me up and ask me back for a role, saying that she didn't want to interfere with whatever I was doing, but that she wanted me for some role or other. She left the door open for me to refuse, but I never did. I was always careful in my personal relationship with her. I would come to rehearsal, get a

15–18. *Three Inventories of Casey Jones*, in duo-concert with José Limón, with May as the engine, José as the engineer, 1939.

pretty good idea of what she was doing, and try to fit in. My movements were in relationship to the movements of the dancers, and I had no set music or number of measures. I think I was the contrast to her, not only as I always was in height and strength, but a balance between her and the younger members. I was like a ballast, a focused center around which things happened, or a Cassandra, walking around the stage silently shouting predictions that no one would believe. I created atmosphere.

Ray Green and May had gone back to San Francisco with Gertrude to establish the San Francisco Dance Theater before she left the Graham company in 1938. Her first venture was a concert of solos, *Of Pioneer Women* (1937), for which Ray wrote the music. Then she toured with José Limón (1939–41). They co-choreographed several works. *So Proudly We Hail* (1940) required a score composed by Ray for two pianos and a choral group. It opened on February 15 at the Veterans Auditorium in San Francisco.

May was appointed as instructor in dance for 1939–40 at the University of California/Berkeley extension division.

"In 1944, nothing much was happening in San Francisco because of World War II. Ray was placed in a language program in Denver. Gert had married Jim Sharp, and they had moved to Portland. But when Sharp died shortly afterward, she went back to New York and founded a studio on University Place. I felt alone, but Gert knew I wanted to continue to be involved in the dance scene, so she suggested I teach. With three students and the sculptress Claire Falkenstein, who had created my mobile for *Suspension* [1943] for my San Francisco Dance Theater, I went to New York, where Gert put us all up in her loft. We founded a new school—the O'Donnell-Shurr Modern Dance Studio.

"Martha asked me [in 1944] to rejoin her company to do major roles and receive guest artist billing. It was with concern that I agreed because I did not want to disrupt my own direction. But it seemed to work out."

Martha's vocabulary and structure had changed once more. Her offer of guest artist status to May was something she had never done for anyone except Erick Hawkins. Dramatic works had entered the repertory: *Deaths and Entrances* (1943), along with *Letter to the World* (1940), *Every Soul Is a Circus* (1939), and *Punch and Judy* (1941).

"Erick [Hawkins] called me. He was always a good friend, and told me that Sophie [Maslow] and Jane [Dudley] were leaving the company and that

Martha needed a mature person who had experience in knowing Martha's way of working."

All the dancers from 1938 had gone, and a new group of young dancers were ready to perform: Pearl Lang, Helen McGehee, and Ethel Winter. May was intrigued with the new challenge, especially in the taking over of Jane Dudley's roles. Dudley was the original dancer in many works, which meant that she had made an actual contribution to them. Learning a role created for someone else would be a new experience for May.

"I no longer took classes in Martha's technique as I evolved my own. Our relationship was professional, the rehearsals set, and I would just go and do the work after she gave me an idea of the quality she wanted. But here was an opportunity to perform with the group as it was getting more established and touring. It would give me a fuller experience.

"Erick called, offering no explanation, as usual, but asked if I would come to Bennington for the summer to work with Martha. The work turned out to be *Appalachian Spring* [1944]. Nor did he tell me about being the Attendant in *Herodiade* [1944]. I had to sense what Martha wanted. I guess she just trusted me. I always wondered why the audience clapped so much at the end of *Herodiade*. I guess it was because, in the role, Martha killed herself!

"I think I saw Martha's role in *Herodiade* as her decision to spend her life in dance. It wasn't an easy dedication at that time, but nothing would have changed her mind. The piece was personal and unique. It was about remembering her life of difficulties, a search within herself danced with such intensity it was almost too much to watch this inner struggle that could destroy her."

In Mallarme's poem, *Herodiade* is confronted in a mirror with her past and her future and is thus left to accept her fate.

"In the dance, Martha met her stage memories with worry, love, and panic. My entrance was to walk toward the darkness of the audience, then make a sudden swirl with my skirt and stop at her feet. There were just the two of us in this work, and in my role, I felt that I was there to ease the way to her fate. She would touch an object on the Noguchi set as if remembering something in her past. I would almost tremble from the work's intensity. The piece never worked for others without us. It was our psychological relationship and our experience together that made it work. It was not a question of steps, or patterns, or anything else you can analyze in a dance. Martha was a great actress, and this was not a role you could pass on. We were the only two who could play that kind of mutual instinctive response.

"As the Pioneer Woman, I never figured out what I was supposed to be looking at as I sat on the porch in *Appalachian Spring*. Of course, Martha never told me. No scenario for me—I just had to look as if I knew what I was doing and what I should be thinking. Up to the last minute, I often wondered if Martha would tell me what to do. She never did. I remember once, when I had no costume, she grabbed a piece of material and wound it around my head. That was it. She had a great sense of costuming.

"Things had changed for me from the thirties when everything I did in the company had to be set. To me, the Pioneer Woman represented the American spirit, its strength in crossing the continent, enduring hardships, but maintaining a vision of the future based upon freedom, hard work, and common sense. That was my choreography for the role.

"At that time, the hardest for me was replacing Jane Dudley. In *Deaths and Entrances* [1943], I tried to imitate her. But she was taller and had different proportions. The costume was too long and I was afraid of tripping. Her exaggerated movements were wonderful for her, terrible for me. But the steps had been set so I was never free to change them. I never felt right in that introspective part.

"In *Letter To the World* [1940], as the Ancestress, I finally broke through to a point where I did a good performance. I was never Jane Dudley, but I grew into the role and it was passable. The Ancestress was a kind of eternal figure. *Punch and Judy* [1941], in which I replaced Jean Erdman, made me feel a bit ridiculous. I was a spectator. All I did was sit in a little stall, watch, and change hats once in a while.

"In *Cave of the Heart* [1946], I did splits around the stage as the Chorus. Imagine doing a split, drawing up, and continuing around the stage! It wasn't easy. I was standing on a Noguchi prop at the opening, and Martha and Erick and Yuriko had their set movements. But, again, knowing where in the music I should come in, it became like a chess game observing the moves of the others and finding a path for myself. In this Medea theme, Martha pitted herself against Erick and beautiful little Yuriko. But again, she never told me what my role was about. She was a rascal.

"That same year [1946], Martha did *Dark Meadow*. I was She of the Earth, or She of the Ground. It was about things coming to life in the spring. There was no rehearsal for me. I wore a kind of knit tube and a brown cape. With my back to the audience, I was instructed by Martha to open my cape and put my arms around the big prop, caressing it. It was a huge penis! Noguchi [Japanese set designer for most of Graham's dances] had made a piece of scenery that looked to me like a stem of asparagus, but it wasn't. It was just like Martha not to tell me about it. My friends told me afterwards what the set was, and I was appalled.

"*Dark Meadow* was followed by *Errand into the Maze* and *Night Journey* in 1947. It got so that I was the eternal symbolic figure, like a kind of angel, in all those later works. Wearing a very long, heavy dress or doing a lot of standing around and waiting, there was not much to do. Critics thought I was badly costumed, and so did I. It wasn't that I had let my technique fall by the way-side; on the contrary, with teaching and creating there was a great deal of Martha's technique left in me and a lot of my own as well. She would build up tension in rehearsals from frustration until the dancers actually shook. Then an explosion would come, and she'd be released to push on.

"She had no trouble knowing what she wanted from the girls in the company, which was lots of energy and scampering around. From the men, she wanted lifting, partnering, and a contrast to the women. But when it came to me, I just had to fit in somehow. It was not like collaborating with her, but more like her putting me into a situation in which I had to sense my way.

"The audience liked *Appalachian Spring*. Martha was young enough to be believed as a bride; Erick was handsome; Merce was a fire-and-brimstone preacher; the music was suitable [Aaron Copland]; the four girls twitted like chicks; and I was the steady influence giving stability and hope to the group. The rhythms of the dances played against each other, especially against the tension that Merce projected as the preacher, and the lyricism of Martha's bride."

Appalachian Spring became the signature piece of the Graham company. Yuriko, a Graham member from 1944 to 1967 who now teaches Graham technique and stages some of her early dances, shares these impressions of May at that time:

"When I joined the group and first saw May, she seemed dignified and so deep in her approach to Martha's choreography. It seemed as if she could almost read her mind. In *Appalachian Spring*, I don't remember Martha showing May what to do, but just telling her where to be on stage in relation to the rest of us. 'Just go around here,' she would say, for instance, as she molded May, like clay, into what she wanted. May understood Martha instinctively. She didn't have to ask her a question. May brought some of her own experience and choreography into Martha's work. This synchronicity between them was also evident in May's role in *Dark Meadow* [1946]. I can still see her in my mind in her strong movements or as the center, holding the action of the story in place. The same intense physicality was there in *Cave of the Heart* [1946]. She was an important contrast to Martha's roles and movements. But in May's role as the servant to Martha in *Hérodiade* [1944], they formed an uncanny bond that has never been duplicated by another cast. No one, but no one, could do what May did on stage.

During rehearsal periods or when we were off stage or on tour, May was not unfriendly, but not close to anyone. She kept her own counsel without being indifferent or aloof. Her dancing was incomparable. Incomparable."

"The big changes in the Graham company," May remembers, "had come in the choreography when men entered the group, Merce Cunningham [1939–45] and Erick Hawkins [1938–50]. Relationships between men and women as characters entered the choreography along with the partnering. The men added a strong movement dimension and were less compliant than the girls."

Hawkins had studied with Harald Kreutzberg and at the School of American Ballet. He was in the early Balanchine ballets staged for the Metropolitan Opera in the 1930s and was a charter member of Ballet Caravan, performing works by Eugene Loring and Lew Christensen. On a program of the First International Dance Festival in New York City (with one night of ballet, one night of modern dance, arranged by Lincoln Kirstein), Hawkins saw Martha dance, and Martha saw Erick. Kirstein gave Hawkins tuition to study at Bennington in 1936, where Martha, Hanya Holm, Doris Humphrey, and Charles Weidman were teaching. He joined the Graham company in 1938 and introduced the ballet barre to Martha's classes. Although the dancers were appalled, Martha managed to incorporate movements from the traditional world into her work and make them her own.

Another change during the 1940s was that the company now toured under the wing of impresario Sol Hurok, and the company appeared on Broadway to huge success.

"I enjoyed the touring and performing," May remembers, "and for having a fuller experience myself. And, of course, there was now a financial income. Martha knew how to impress people with money, and she knew how to be ruthless when she had to be.

"Martha was fascinated with Erick. He was young and handsome. He had done two little dances for a summer program that Louis didn't think worth much. We could see changes in Martha's attention from Louis to Erick and maneuvered around these shifts in attraction. The musicians at that summer performance at New London, Connecticut, would not permit us rehearsal overtime, and either Louis' or Erick's piece had to go. It was a hard decision for Martha, but she chose Erick's piece to be performed. The girls felt sorry for Louis and went to his cabin to give him coffee cake and cookies. The atmosphere became quite dark. Louis was smart enough to accept the choice. But suddenly he was an old man, and it was kind of pathetic.

"By 1948, there were turning points in many other ways. Louis left after the premiere of *Diversion of Angels,* despite Martha's pleading for him to stay. The relationship between Martha and Erick had gotten deeper, and she talked to me about it, asking if she should marry him. He was thirty-nine, and she was fifty-four. I replied that age shouldn't stop her. For all we knew, our lives could end without notice in an accident crossing the street and that we should take whatever happiness we could. Martha and Erick drove to Santa Fe the next day and were married by a Presbyterian minister."

Erick was an influence on Martha as she began her works on Greek myths. He had been a student of Greek literature at Harvard and had planned to do many of the Greek works himself.

"I remember that Erick wanted more visibility on stage and had performed a work that Martha had presented during a Broadway season. But he never received very good reviews. Finally, the group became the 'Martha Graham and Company with Erick Hawkins' as soloist.

"But Erick had become restless. He felt held back by Martha and his own bad reviews on Broadway. He felt that the critics were against him because of her. She choreographed the King Lear story for him as *Eye of Anguish* [1950] for the European tour. It was not successful. It was possible that Martha, who had always choreographed major roles about women, was not able to choreograph as well for men.

"In 1950, Martha had been offered a Paris/London season, and she asked me, although I was busy with my own company and choreography, to go. I had billing after Martha and Erick on every program.

"Martha made it clear that the tour depended upon my going since she couldn't fill my roles with anyone else. She even sent Erick to coax me. I always liked Erick. I told her that I wouldn't fly in a plane. I felt that the European trip would not work for me and that it was time for me to leave. I told Martha: 'I need my time now. You don't need me. You're there and it's already possibly too late for me.' She was very upset but didn't lose her temper. She just seethed and was very annoyed. That's when she sent Erick over to see me about the tour. They got me a ticket on the *Queen Mary*.

"When I arrived in Paris, on the first night the curtain went up two hours late. Martha was in a great state of frustration and had slammed herself down on the floor and tore cartilage in her knee. Bethsabee de Rothschild gave us a reception in her townhouse after the performance, but by the time we got to the theater the next day, we found that the concerts were canceled. Martha was unable to dance on the programs. The public wanted to see only her. Pearl Lang had hurt her foot earlier, as well. Ticket sales had slumped because of Martha's injury, and the rest of the engagement was canceled. I made the best of it by getting around to see things by using the subway. I made the best of it. Everyone hoped that in the next stop in London, that all would be well. But it was not to be."

May had crossed the English Channel to London and everyone hoped that Martha would soon be able to perform. Erick, convinced that Martha was faking the injury to hurt him, left her to stay in another place. "Martha called a meeting of the company one morning in the lobby where drinks were sold during intervals of the performance. The smell of stale smoke and cigarette butts in the ashtrays were the props for the dismal news. Martha, in a terrible state, told us that there were to be no more performances and that she had arranged our return passage. Actually, I believed that Martha had created the Lear work for him so he would stay with her and be recognized in Europe.

"It was depressing for all of us. Hawkins had considered himself Martha's equal, but according to the public and the press, he was not. Every work he had done on his own was unsuccessful. He had begun to give in to his homosexual tendencies. The company experienced a lot of tension backstage. There were tears, fear, and hysterics. I told Martha it was all just an incident in her big career and that all would be regained. We each kissed her, and I felt sorry for her."

Erick, as the business manager of the company, had created a great deal of dissension. Finally, he divided the company money, left a note, and disappeared. He continued to create his own choreography and company afterwards. Martha went to the Southwest to recover and apply her own weight-lifting therapy to her injury. Eventually, she recovered.

"My last performance with the company was in *Hérodiade*. I felt it was a suitable ending for us both. I had always been placed in the same mold by Martha and felt that it was time to assume my responsibility to my own work and company. Years later, when I visited a much older Martha backstage as she watched her company rehearse from her chair on stage right, she recognized me and with affection said, 'My May.' It was said from her heart."

Seven Beginning a Choreographic Career

Before May rejoined the Graham company (1944–53) and witnessed all the company traumas, she had begun a choreographic life of her own.

"The summer of 1937," she remembers, "when Gert and I took the ship to California to visit my folks, we were invited to Betty Horst's studio to introduce modern dance. Betty had been one of the leading dancers with Denishawn and had a school in San Francisco. When the Graham company was on tour in San Francisco, Betty Horst had asked Martha for two dancers to teach the technique. About two weeks before we were to return to New York and the company, Betty Horst asked us to give a demonstration at a dinner in her studio. I was introduced to Ray Green after the demonstration. He had just returned from two years in Europe, having won the George Ladd Prix de Paris in 1935, awarded by the University of California/Berkeley to study modern music. Instead of staying in Paris, he wandered all over the continent to explore and observe. He studied briefly with Darius Milaud and Nadia Boulanger and conducting with Pierre Monteux." But, disappointed with their pedagogical approach, went his own way, and like May, wanted to explore new territory.

He had written a piece for modern dancer Ann Mundstock, who had come from the German school and was interested in writing more music for dance.

"I was impressed with someone who had walked all over Europe for two years seeking new music. I liked his independence. We hit it off right away. He watched our classes, and I asked him if he could compose a piece for me. I also asked him if he would compose a piece for Martha. He said he would love to do that. He had his eye on me, and I had my eye on him!"

Raymond Burns Green was born September 13, 1908, in Avalon, Missouri, into a musical family. His father trained, rehearsed, and wrote music for the local choir. Ray learned how to sight-read inner parts, the melody, and everything else in a score before he could do the multiplication tables. By the time he was ten years old, he could notate music without having had any formal musical education. While in grade school, he created pieces for piano, and, when the family moved to California, he began his formal musical training at the age of fourteen. Upon graduating from high school, and with money earned in small jobs, Green entered the San Francisco Conservatory of Music (1927–33), where he was instructed in harmony and ear-training. He studied piano privately with a conservatory staff member, and his progress in the classes of Ernest Bloch (1880–1959) in analytical form and harmony by writing compositions in various forms earned him a scholarship in 1928. At the conservatory, Green was given the Carnegie Foundation Award for composition study (1930–31). The award enabled him to continue his study in orchestration, composition, and forms with Albert Elkus at the University of California (1933–35). By then, Green had written several compositions and was considered a promising composer.

"Ray's first composition for me [for two pianos and a choral group] was *Of Pioneer Women,* and it was my response to all the political turmoil in the East. I considered the interest in communism to be just a trend. The piece was a reaffirmation of my feelings about American freedom. I was idealistic about my country.

"Earlier I had composed a piece called *Prologue* for the Horst composition class using Martha's technique. It was a Greek prologue. Martha and Louis gave me a book called *The Greek Way,* which they inscribed to me. This was long before Martha did her works based on Greek myths, which were to come [in the 1940s and 1950s], but she remembered my piece.

"Gert and I returned to New York at the end of the summer of 1937. Louis asked me about Ray's music. Martha knew Ray had written a work for me, and she was looking for a new piece to open at Bennington. She knew of Ray's background and commissioned him to compose the music for her *American Document* [1938, for two pianos and drums]. It was the first piece in which Erick Hawkins danced.

"The Bennington commission for Martha's dance gave Ray $125, enough money to buy an old green Ford coupe. So Gert and I got into his car and set off for California. By the time we got to Santa Fe, Ray and I had decided to get married, and we did. Right then! An Indian jeweler made our rings for fifty cents each. They were little silver bands."

The pioneer spirit in both of them drove their efforts to find a path together. California, where Isadora Duncan, Loie Fuller, and Ruth St. Denis had their dancing roots, was the place the Greens returned to find theirs.

"When I left the Graham company in 1938, I felt that I could better explore my choreography away from the East. When we got to San Francisco, Gert, Ray, and I were broke and had to think about how to make a living. Gertrude's brother was an agent. Bob Hope, the comedian, was one of his clients. Her brother gave us some money. Ray's sister and brother-in-law, whose work took them on the road, gave Ray and me their San Francisco apartment. Ray got a commission to write a piece for the 1939 San Francisco Fair, which he called *Processional Dance for Symphonic Band,* and Gert got a job with a theater outfit. She was so good at teaching beginners; I looked for a few students for her, and Ray had his university contacts. We found a studio and established the San Francisco Dance Theater.

"I did a solo concert in 1940. By then, Ray and I had our own apartment on Sutter Street, where I worked out all the choreography. Ray found work as choral director of the Northern California Chorus, a division of the Federal Music Project of the Works Progress Administration [WPA]. He orchestrated his work and had a group of copyists to assist him. He was also put in charge of a chorus that gave school performances. The spirit of America was everywhere. *So Proudly We Hail* was the name of our new work, and it included *Of Pioneer Women.* It was a full evening of thirteen solos.

"Everything went wrong in the beginning. The theater manager wanted more money at the last minute and refused to open the curtain. When I thought of all the solo dances I was going to do, I wondered why I was doing it! But I got through it with good reviews."

Alfred Frankenstein, a San Francisco critic, called her "one of the most perfectly trained modern dancers in America, destined to carry on in the work of the great artist, Graham, whose discipline she clearly revealed."

Nell Silva of *Peoples World,* however, saw May as having "her own free, flowing quality, not in the static style of Martha Graham." The "River of Desolation" section in *So Proudly We Hail* received special acclaim.

The concert took place in the Veterans Auditorium, February 15, 1940, in San Francisco. May was invited to repeat the program in Oakland at Mills College and at Bennington in the summer of 1940. That same year at Mills College, Merce Cunningham represented Martha; José Limón represented Doris Humphrey. Limón was choreographing his *War Lyrics* and needed a strong female lead. He chose May because he had seen her perform at Mills in Oakland.

"José had an almost Aztec-like face with high cheekbones, a strong nose and chin, and a wonderful physique. At the end of the summer, he asked if he could work with me in San Francisco. By then, Doris [Humphrey] and Charles [Weidman] were breaking up, and José wasn't sure of his future. I told him we had nothing to offer and just about paid the rent. All we had was a dance studio across the hall from our living room. I forgot about the whole thing.

"One day, after Gert and I had opened the studio, a telegram arrived, saying: 'I'm arriving . . . José.' He arrived penniless and slept on a cot in our studio. We gave him meals. José had done a few works on his own when he worked with Doris and Charles. He was broken up about the split between Doris and Charles, although he didn't talk much about it. He played sad pieces on the piano but was jolly on the surface. He was sorrowing underneath. We lost ourselves in work.

"José had done a piece for the 1939 World's Fair called *Casey Jones*. We became a team using that piece. José was the engineer, and I was the engine! It was a romp that we enjoyed, complete with José dancing with an oil can. We played little towns, mostly for farm people who didn't know a thing about modern dance. We choreographed *This Story Is Legend,* a romantic interpretation of Hernando de Soto's discovery of the Mississippi, based on a poem of William Carlos Williams. I had done a piece at Berkeley, *Theme and Variations,* which we reworked to become a duet. We did our solos as well. Our full program was called *On American Themes* [1941] to Ray's music [for spoken voice, trumpet, piano, and drums]. It consisted of 'Curtain Raiser,' 'This Story Is Legend,' 'War Lyrics,' and 'Three Inventories of Casey Jones.' We opened in Seattle Repertory Playhouse, March 23, 1941.

"We performed jointly with these programs for three years [1940–42] with some performances in larger towns: San Francisco, Portland, Seattle, Los Angeles, Santa Barbara, Detroit, and then New York."

Dancers [O'Donnell and José Limón] present vigorous ideas in recital.

Agile technique of duo applauded, even cheered.
—Headlines, Arthur Fried, *San Francisco Examiner,* 1941

"Then, Doris wanted José to come back to her company in New York, which was a move that I had expected. But when he returned, he found that his association with the Humphrey-Weidman company had ended. He took the train back to San Francisco and was available and anxious to choreograph.

"Ray introduced Gert to a friend, Jim Sharp, who was in charge of the WPA art program. They married and moved to Portland, where she got her master's in dance.

"During 1940, 1941, and 1942, as José and I toured up and down the coast, Ray was our composer and manager. He drove our green coupe loaded with costumes, scenery, and personal luggage.

"José and I had a wonderful way of working together as partners. We would try various things separately, and he or I would say that it was good. Then we would do it together. We made quite a sensation as a team because we were both strong, and that part of the country had seen little modern dance. José's *War Lyrics,* which he choreographed for Mills College, was put on our program as *Three Women.* One role was that of a nurse; another, a wife; and the third, a prostitute. I was all three women, while José was the male in each section. My *Theme and Variations* was our duet in a high style of formality. José had the quality for this naturally, along with his great dignity, so it was a suitable work for both us.

"It was a heady time, exciting, and as a group, we felt full of promise. But José was disturbed. He kept getting letters from the East. The breakup between Charles and Doris was definite."

Pauline Lawrence, who managed the Humphrey-Weidman studio, came to the West Coast. In 1941, Pauline and José were married, with Ray and May as witnesses. They gave the couple a wedding luncheon and their car for a honeymoon trip. Pauline returned to New York. José reminisces:

May and I worked well together. We made a handsome team. We were eager to make further progress. There was constant discussion. Ideas were presented, examined, discarded, accepted, deferred. This went on endlessly, from morning to night, in the studio and even at meals. The air was charged with excitement and expectation. We stimulated one another to a high degree. We were very serious young people, yet we had moments of great good humor. All of us had a healthy sense of irony and a fine appreciation of the absurd and the bawdy. We needed this. We lived in a world perched precariously on the brink of chaos and disaster. At any moment our fine plans, our precious artistic aspirations, and our entire lives might topple over the edge.

—excerpt from *An Unfinished Memoir* (© 1998 by José Limón and reprinted by permission of Wesleyan University Press)

When the team finished their remaining concerts in 1942, the three returned to New York to do a few concerts that were not as well received as they had been in the West. The tour ended in Detroit at the YMHA (Young Men's Hebrew Association) and in a performance at the Humphrey-Weidman Studio Theater in New York. Their success was moderate. Ray and May returned to their Post Street studio in San Francisco and established the May O'Donnell Dance Company without José, who had his following in the East and an audience built over the years at Bennington.

"I felt that it was best for him to work under the artistic direction of Doris. For myself, I wanted to go it alone. It was discouraging not to get the reviews we had gotten in the West. It was time for me to reevaluate my work."

That reevaluation led to what would become one of the first abstract modern dance works and her signature piece, *Suspension* (1943).

Limón, who was born in Mexico, registered as an alien resident and was drafted. Green was drafted as well. Now, back in her studio in California without Ray, May began work on her new piece.

"One day, alone on a mountaintop, I saw a plane and a ship below me and realized there is no such thing as up or down. The world, in the midst of World War II, was crazy, with no reason for man's inhumanity. I thought that man could not be so important in the big picture. We have to trust, I thought, in a bigger law of nature that seems to hold the universe together in a kind of balance. Things move in their own orbit and yet hold their own kind of energy and design.

"I was fascinated with mobiles, which seemed to be related to the basic law of balance in our bodies. I was beginning to let go of despair. Ray, who was now appointed Instructor of Music Reconditioning in Denver at Fort Logan Convalescent Hospital of the Army Air Corps, sent me the music according to my counts. His music was an experiment with sound for percussion and piano, sometimes ahead of me a few measures, but eventually a fine collaboration. It had just the right amount of emotional pull."

Dick Moore, a friend and poet, upon seeing the work in a studio performance, borrowing from T. S. Eliot's *Four Quartets,* wrote: "at the still point of the turning world, there the dance is." The work with parts that seemed suspended in time and space received its name—*Suspension.* It opened to an audience of twenty-five, the full studio capacity, on February 2, 1943, the same day that Ray was drafted. Later the work was performed at the California School of Fine Arts and at the San Francisco Museum of Art. A distinctive mobile by Claire Falkenstein was used for the performance. José had left two boxes as props in the studio.

"The boxes enabled me to do upside-down things, a feeling I wanted in the piece."

The work was considered an oddity but later recognized as unique. Don McDonagh, dance critic for the *New York Times,* reviewing it at a performance at Jacob's Pillow, July 21, 1968, danced by Norman Walker Company in 1968 and again in 1975, found that: "When it saw the light of theater in 1943, it was ahead of its time. It was revolutionary in its quiet way."

San Francisco was a worried city in the early 1940s. Japanese bombs and air raids were a constant threat. Ray was concerned for May's safety and suggested she go back to New York. Shurr—who had returned to New York in 1942 after the untimely death of her husband—and May now became founders of the O'Donnell-Shurr Dance Studio, not knowing what was to come next. Then three dancers from May's group in San Francisco showed up. Shurr, with her customary problem-solving ability, put them all up. Students Elizabeth Good and Nancy Land were in New York, and with a few new students, May was ready to restage *Suspension.*

May auditioned for the Ninety-second Street YMHA dance series and was

19–22. "DeSoto" and "Mississippi" from *This Story Is Legend*, May and José, 1941.

invited to appear in a joint program with Nina Fonaroff. The program in-
cluded the first New York performance of *Suspension* and *Of Pioneer Women*.
The date was April 29, 1945, and the performance included an added solo by
May on the boxes of the *Suspension* scenery.

"One day, when lighting director Jean Rosenthal happened to come to the
studio, she saw a rehearsal of *Suspension* and offered to light it for me. That
was a great honor and the piece received some interesting reviews."

Graham saw the performance and remarked that her dancers who had presented choreography in the series had embarrassed her, except for May and
her *Suspension*. Ruby Gluck Zimmerman, one of the dancers in *Suspension*,
offers this impression of working with May:

"I was still in high school when I first joined the May O'Donnell and Her
Dance Company in 1949. My good grades reflected the time I spent studying
and rehearsing. As far as I remember, I was the first 'young one' in the company. It was hard work, but I loved it. We were a big family. Gertrude Shurr was
our den mother, our go-between with May, who was held in awe, on a pedestal.
I remember May saying that she created her dances ON us. I remember, as
well, when Charles Ives came to observe a rehearsal. But our greatest thrill
was in performing *Suspension*, May's masterpiece. I was honored to have taken
part and to have been in the dance world during those wonderful years."

Eight Returning to the Graham Company

In 1944, with May now back in New York, the time was right for her to return to the Graham company, while still managing her own studio and company. From 1942 to 1945, it would be called May O'Donnell's Dance Company.

It was the beginning of Graham's period of creating ballets based upon Greek myths, influenced not only by Hawkins but also by Joseph Campbell, a renowned authority on mythology who was married to Graham dancer Jean Erdman.

"Now I felt more isolated, cast into the same mold in every role and used as a foil for Martha. But I never made a personal demand on her. I realized, especially when she began to have men in the company, that she was pushed by people complaining and wanting this and that. I never got into that with her. It would be better not to. Very often, especially in the early days, with all the rehearsals, I remembered that some of the dancers would get depressed and exhausted. Tempers were on edge. When we got to a dress rehearsal and had only that day to stage and have a tech rehearsal [technical run-through with lights and music], she'd take one look at the work and say: 'It's going to be a failure.' But she was on that upgrade and knew how to get the right support. She felt political trends and knew how to take advantage of them. She was in good health and knew how to impress people and how to be ruthless when she had to be. She said herself that she was lucky, but she knew that she was being astute.

"I asked myself if it was worth it. If you don't like it, I told myself, then get out. If you're going to stay, keep quiet and don't complain. I kept my mouth shut. I knew from experience that there would sometimes be little time to operate and that no one would be satisfied with what they had to do. Everyone is on your neck and you wonder if it's all worth it. It's hard.

23. Graham with May as the "Pioneer Woman" in *Appalachian Spring,* 1944.

"Martha and Erick were living together, and he was still in the company [1945–50] but anxious to do his own work. With support from Martha, he had a studio where he taught and choreographed. He had formed his own company in the 1940s, and he would continue to choreograph and perform until his death in 1994.

"Erick asked me to share a performance with him. It was only one performance in which I performed two solo works to Ray's *Theme and Variations* and

24. Original cast, *Appalachian Spring*, 1944; *top to right*: Merce Cunningham, May O'Donnell, Erick Hawkins, Martha Graham.

Rondo Running Set [a work that would become his *Kentucky Mountain Running Set* in 1946]. Erick had his own ideas, mainly influenced by the Southwest from where he came, that were different from mine. So we were an interesting contrast."

That one performance took place at Lindenwood College, in St. Charles, Missouri, on April 16, 1945.

May was teaching at the art workshop in an adult education program as

25. May (*standing*) with Graham in her *Cave of the Heart*, 1946.

26. May leaning backward in Graham's *Dark Meadow,* 1946.

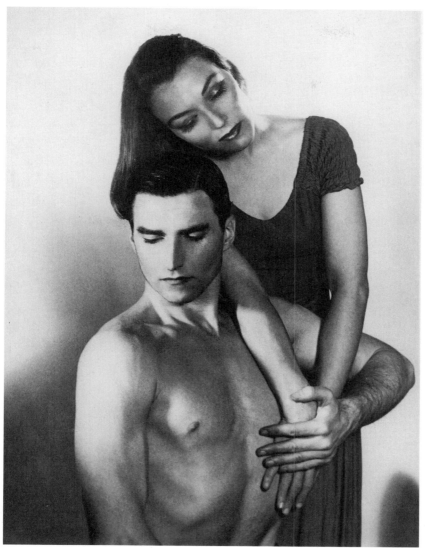

27. May and Erick Hawkins in a studio shot, 1945.

28. Erick Hawkins and May in *Theme and Variations,* from their one concert, 1945.

29. May in her *Celtic Ritual,* 1949.

30. May in her *Horizon Song,* Jacob's Pillow, 1949.

well as spending more rehearsal time on Martha's programs. "I felt less and less like going on the European trip, in 1951, but when Erick had called me saying that I couldn't be replaced, I went and was finished with the company for good by 1953."

Ray had continued the research into music therapy that he had begun in Colorado after the war, becoming chief of music for the Veterans Administration in Washington, D.C. He was responsible for organizing a music therapy program for returning soldiers. Under the G.I. Bill of Rights, Green obtained his bachelor of arts degree at Columbia University.

With Karl Menninger, the renowned psychiatrist, Ray pioneered Music by Prescription. Ray gave instrumental or choral instruction to veterans with orthopedic and emotional problems to help them return to muscular and mental health. He became cofounder and first president of the National Association for Music Therapy. When he resigned in 1948, he became executive secretary of the American Music Center, a position he held until 1961. In 1951, he founded his own publishing house, the American Music Edition, to promote American composers.

"My first group of dancers in 1945 was technically limited, but because they went through every inch of a program with me, they more than made up for their technical limitations. On my own, I didn't work like Martha, using the people in the company. In my technique, I used the contraction-and-release principle but explored for myself what I could feel was secure and sincere.

"The hardest part always was finding the starting point upon which I could build. I experimented and experimented, trying things this way and then that way, until it looked right. I could never just walk into the studio for rehearsal and walk out with a finished dance. I think a lot of Horst's teaching still remained with me in wanting something personal and individual. His contribution to me in finding structure and content was inestimable. He influenced the entire modern dance movement with his teaching of music and dance composition. He instilled the need for structure and deep intent.

"By 1949, I created my second dance company, May O'Donnell and Her Dance Company. Our debut performance took place at a gala at the Jewish Community Center in Detroit, February 1949, after a concert at Bennett Junior College at Millbrook, New York."

That same year and just as busy, Ray received a glowing review for his *Festi-*

val Fugues: An American Toccata from Glenn Dillard Gunn of the *Washington Times-Herald*: "Let it be said at once that this set of two preludes and three fugues is one of the most important contemporary piano works produced in any land."

"When I returned to New York, two students of Mary Ann Wells—the ballet teacher who was so open to new ideas and who had invited Gert and me to teach in San Francisco—arrived wanting to know more about modern dance. They were Robert Joffrey and Gerald Arpino. [Later, they became founders of the Joffrey Ballet and Joffrey Ballet of Chicago.] They were both very talented, and I took them into my company. Bob was very organized; Jerry was exuberant; and the two were a good team."

The year 1949 became highly successful for the company and included her: *Celtic Ritual* (music by Henry Cowell), *Horizon Song* (Green), *Praeludium* (Green), *Fanfare in Jig Time* (Green), *Fortress of Tragedy* (Green), and *Forsaken Gardens* (Green).

The professional relationship begun in 1937 between Ray and May was to last a lifetime.

"It wasn't always easy, but I believe that we are in a mystery called life that is beyond our understanding. It's not something you can touch or investigate beyond your own experience. But there is a creative force that surrounds us that we can use and call upon. You can feel it in dance—it's something beyond. Ray and I never made personal demands of any kind of each other. His recognition as a composer didn't change his personality, which was direct and giving. You might say we had a fortunate life together, but it was more a question of keeping free in the way we related to each other, as much as keeping freedom in our work."

They were independent and interdependent for better or worse.

Nine The 1950s

"We found the 1950s a wonderful time. For only five hundred dollars, we could produce an entire concert," May remembered. "People were responsive to all kinds of dance. And I had those wonderful dancers during that period: Robert Joffrey, Gerald Arpino, Norman Walker, Bill Luther, Jonathan Watts, Mabel Robinson, Arthur Mitchell, and others. Of course, no sooner were they trained and experienced, I lost them to Graham or New York City Ballet, where they could be paid for rehearsals and performances."

May's company appeared annually in New York City with premieres each season opening with *Magic Ceremony* to music of Henry Cowell (1950) and *Ritual of Transition* to music of Edgard Varese (1951). *Ritual* opened at Boston Dance Theater Associates, Inc., on March 1 and 2. In the *Boston Traveler,* Cameron Dewar commented: "Miss O'Donnell has few peers in any dance form. Until recently Miss O'Donnell was associated with Martha Graham. But she seems to have gone on and upward from the technique of Miss Graham taking the best and adding her own excellent sense of values and invention."

In 1952, at the Kauffman Auditorium at New York's YMHA, the performance included *Dance Sonata #1* (Green); *Act of Renunciation,* with music of Carl Ruggles; *Spell of Silence,* to music of Charles Ives's *Unanswered Question;* and *The Queen's Obsession,* with music by Green and based on Shakespeare's *Macbeth.* John Martin described this performance in the April 20, 1952, *New York Times*: "These thirteen youngsters work together with wonderful unity, with probably the greatest realization of true modern dance virtuosity that we have yet seen, with honesty of feeling, with theatrical awareness and with a discipline that is truly professional in the best use of the word."

The Queen's Obsession was a spectacular solo for May. But the biggest success of the decade was *Dance Sonata #1* (1952). It premiered at the Ninety-second Street YMHA and was done at first without music and then to music by Charles Jones and then by Ray Green.

"I liked the idea of a sonata form because it has various sections which are contrasting. The form was a prelude, a scherzo, an intermezzo, and mixed accents coming at different times." It had a rousing section for boys and the critics said that May had built a company that could tear through space with a maximum of dynamic excitement.

Bethsabee de Rothschild had established a foundation and produced a program titled "The American Dance Festival" at the Alvin Theater on Broadway, April 14–19, in 1953. May was one of her "new" choreographers, and her company received union-scale wages. They felt as if they had arrived. At that season on Broadway, Limón, Humphrey, Graham, Pearl Lang, Cunningham, Helen McGehee, and Charles Weidman appeared along with others.

Three performances scheduled in 1953—at the Central High School of Needle Trades in New York, the Philadelphia Art Alliance, and Irvine Auditorium at the University of Pennsylvania—received excellent reviews that won them the season at the American Dance Festival on Broadway.

31. *Left to right*: Jonathan Watts, Robert Joffrey, Gerald Arpino, Arthur Yahiro rehearsing *Ritual of Transition*, 1951.

Concertino, to music by Charles Jones, was a 1953 offering, as was *Dance Sonata* by Green. The premiere of *Incredible Adventure* (1954), to music of Paul Bowles, opened at Hunter College Playhouse in New York City, March 5 and 6, 1955. The work was encouraged by Louis Horst. *Legendary Forest* (1954), to music of Eugene Hemmer, opened at Hunter College Playhouse, January 9 and 10.

"It was a piece that Louis Horst also liked very much, although it was different from my big, heroic style. It was like a morality play, almost medieval. The music had a fairy tale feel to it."

Dance Concerto (1954), to Béla Bartok's music, created the same year, became one of her most important works. The work had a dramatic solo. It was the exploration in ritual form of the visions, pressures, doubts, discoveries, and joys that characterize the artist's creative process. For the ensemble, May created a vivid design, strong, and emotionally compulsive, as the dancers leapt, fell, rolled, spinned, and surged across the stage. Its excitement was hair-raising.

"When I was asked to do *Dance Concerto* (Béla Bartok) at the American Dance Festival in Connecticut that summer, I refused because they asked me to change the music because of union rules concerning the orchestra. The musicians were assembled for Graham, Humphrey, and Limón, and my combination of sounds would have cost more money. I said 'no' because artistically it would not have been right."

Lilacs and Portals (1956), with music by Charles Ruggles, and *Illuminations* (1956), to the music of J. S. Bach, were next premiered. A highlight for May was an appearance with the company, on April 14, 1956, at the Brooklyn Academy of Music with the Brooklyn Philharmonia, under the direction of conductor Siegfried Landau. It was the first performance of *Dance Concerto* (Bach) to live music, and of *Illuminations* to his Brandenburg Concerto.

"*Illuminations* was a very good piece, and people loved it. But the first performance lets you know that you should do something about it. Although it was very much praised, I never did it again. I never redid it, either. It was a big piece and a long one, but I was always a little leery about using music of the past. I felt a responsibility to use the music of my own time. But as I look back, the performance I most enjoyed was this one, since I had live music and enough room to dance full out."

32. May in *The Queen's Obsession*, 1952.

33. May in *Dance Concerto*, 1954.

34. May in *Legendary Forest*, 1954.

35. May in
Illuminations,
1956.

The New York "Y" (1958) was once again the site for May's company in premiere: *Dance Sonata #2* (Green); *Drift* (Anton Webern); and *The Threshold* (Léon Kirschner).

Inventions (Green); *Footfalls Echo in Memory* (Bartok); *Sonata in D* (Green); and *Pelléas and Melisande* (Carl Ruggles) ended the 1959 season.

The Queen's Obsession (1959 version) had May solo-walking at Utah State University at Logan, Utah, along with *The Haunted* (Green). *Dance Energies* (Green) had its premiere at Philadelphia Dance Academy on March 9, and at the YMHA in New York on March 15, 1959. The Hertz Memorial Auditorium in Berkeley, California, presented the company in the summers of 1959, 1960, and 1961. California appearances in 1959 included University of California (July 10); Stanford University (July 11); San Jose State (summer festival

36. *Left to right:* Rachel Yocum, Gertrude Shurr, and May O'Donnell strolling in Washington, D.C., 1950s.

of the arts); Daily Auditorium (July 13); Schoenberg Hall, UCLA, Los Angeles (July 15). Each festival concluded with a performance by the company.

"This was our barnstorming period when we performed anywhere and in any circumstance. The company ate in the cafeterias of the school where we played and slept in the dorms whenever the performances were college-sponsored. There were chaperones, but that made no difference to the boys—Jerry, Bill and Robert—who loved to disappear into town. Some of the performances were outdoors. Parents drove us from concert site to site or we took trains and buses. It was much like Martha's early period. We had little money. Ray managed us somehow, but modern dance had taken hold and the colleges wanted to know more and more about it in workshops and concerts."

The New York studio was then at Fifty-sixth Street, where May had created

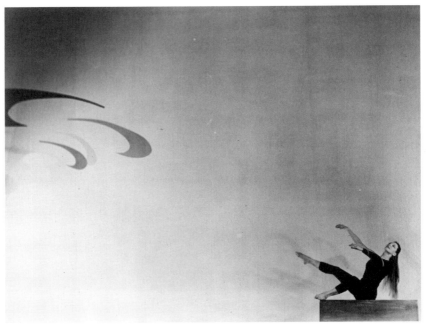

37. May in *Suspension,* restaged at the Ninety-second Street "Y," 1950s.

Dance Sonata #2. The section for men gave Joffrey and Arpino important exposure. Later, Norman Walker and Jonathan Watts danced those roles.

"Norman was a wonderful person to work with because he was so anxious and so alive; he just ate up everything. Before you suggested something, he was ready to try it. He was one of my best studio cleaners. Seriously, I can tell by the way a student cleans a studio if they are going to be the best dancers. They take responsibility! Mabel Leslie, who headed the Art Workshop, where I once taught, helped me finance the concerts. She would give me five hundred dollars to go ahead with a performance. 'You can pay me back out of the box office,' she would say. While five hundred dollars doesn't seem like much now, it was the equivalent to about $2,500 today. I always paid her back.

"And once again, Mabel Leslie came to our rescue in the mid-fifties when we had to move the studio once more. She also needed space and shared a lovely, big, expensive studio with us. It had windows overlooking Fifth Avenue. There we remained until the early seventies. It was also there that I taught the dance program for Mills College, in New York, which was on Fifth Avenue at that time.

"But there was always that push in getting money together year after year. Despite my wonderful reviews in the 1950s, there was still little money available for modern dance. If there was any, it seemed to go to Martha, José, or Doris. I thought I should take a rest and retire from dancing and just teach. I was tired. So many things can go wrong when you prepare for a concert. The lighting, the costumes. And yet, you have to perform no matter what. There were little cults that my good reviews could not influence. John Martin in the *New York Times* gave my first concert at the YMHA a terrific review, but then— and I still can't believe it—when I called to offer him tickets and he said that he would never miss one of my concerts, he said he couldn't write them up because they were Off Broadway!

"I felt that you just didn't call a critic about your work. It should speak for itself. Now, I hear that if a review is not good, the critic is called up! I was probably too standoffish or didn't have a big enough staff for a fund-raiser or press agent. But I have no regrets."

Recognition was yet to come. With no calls made.

Gerald Arpino reminisces about his experiences as a dancer with May O'Donnell during this time:

"I remember my days with May O'Donnell as one of the most fortunate and beautiful times in my life. Mary Ann Wells, my teacher in Seattle, always gave us a Graham warm-up before we went to the barre, so May's centered and strong technique was a continuation of what I knew was right for me.

38. Student rehearsal for *Dance Sonata #2,* in May's studio, 1958.

"May was beautiful and statuesque, and her inspiration extended into my own choreography, especially in my *Light Rain*." Gerald Arpino, artistic director of Joffrey Ballet Chicago, was a member of O'Donnell's company from 1952 to 1954. He became a dancer on Broadway, chief choreographer of the Joffrey Ballet, and the distinguished creator of many works. He co-directed the American Ballet Center in New York with Robert Joffrey, providing most of the dancers in the Joffrey Ballet, 1954 through the 1970s.

Lida Nelson Smith recalls: "I danced with the May O'Donnell Concert Dance Company from 1955 to 1959 as Lida Witsel. May was featured in her stirring dramatic work *Dance Concerto,* set to Bartok's violin concerto. Her slow rise from a seated position at the start of the dance is permanently etched in my memory. May's *Legendary Forest,* inspired by tapestries in the Cloisters [a museum of medieval art affiliated with the Metropolitan Art Museum in New York], by contrast was swift, light, and joyous. In another dramatic work, *Drift,* set to the music of Anton Weber, May contrasted neurotic shapes of the adult world, inspired by the twisted shapes of driftwood, with the innocent world of the child.

"In the summer of 1959, we taught a workshop at the University of California in Berkeley, followed by performances there and a short tour. My years in the company were exciting. May's swiftly moving classes were conducted using only a small drum and her rich voice; her inspired rehearsals fueled by her seemingly endless and rich movement invention. If there every was a pure person dedicated entirely to her art, it had to have been May O'Donnell. For those of us fortunate enough to have worked with her, it was an unforgettable experience."

Ten The 1960s and London

The beginning of the 1960s found May tired and philosophical. But the professional collaboration and personal relationship between May and her composer husband, Ray, would last throughout their lives, resulting in separate, as well as collaborative works.

"I believe in movement, all kinds of movement, and that when we move, there is progress. No, not the kind of movement that causes destruction, for it always amazed me that humans can be so stupid. But creation and movement can cause change for good. We have to stay creative, in some way, our entire lives. The biggest joy is in awakening that creative force in a student. You can tell those who will just be good at dance and the others to whom dance means everything."

Separations between the two because of individual engagements caused anxiety. Ray, in demand as a famous and glamorous artist, attracted women whom May described as "having nothing to do. If there were any affairs, I ignored them and even felt sorry for those few, because I knew that Ray and I had a strong love for each other."

On August 3, 1952, Ray wrote May this letter from Cheyenne, Wyoming, where he was on one of his many trips as a guest artist, composer, teacher, or lecturer:

> May, My Angel Love. This is the most difficult leave-taking of all. Lucky for me that it was in the car going back to the motel because of my tears and wet eyes. I poked along in the right lane all the way back and my weeping for you, my love angel, finally came to a halt after a torrent of tears. I cannot live without you . . . Forever, Ray.

May never explained the circumstances that prompted the letter, but she kept it and asked that it be put into her casket. It was.

In 1957, the first music grant of $210,000 was awarded to Green to commission composers. It resulted in the American Music Center Commissioning Series. In 1961, he was given a presidential citation by the National Federation of Music Clubs in recognition of his distinguished contributions to the musical life of the nation. His publishing house, American Music Edition, brought out the works of American composers Paul Bowles and Carl Ruggles, among others. Books A and B in the Ray Green Piano Books for Young Pianists series, and books C and D completed the series in 1960–61.

In 1961, May's company performed with the Knoxville Symphony Orchestra in Tennessee. David Van Vector conducted the premiere of his music for May's premiere of *Dance Contrasts with Three Dancers* and conducted Bartok's music for *Dance Concerto* on February 21.

Green's *Sunday Sing Symphony* and May's work with the same name had their world premiere with the Kansas City Philharmonic under the direction of Hans Schweiger at the Thirty-first Biennial Convention of the National Federation of Music Clubs on April 26, 1961. This collaborative work was based on early hymn tunes.

"I looked at a lot of gravestones on some of the early graves that had some marvelous writing on them. I tried to capture some of the quality, the feeling of life and death in an early American period. Ray also did a lot of research. His father had written a few pieces for Sunday school, and Ray had spent time in Texas at what they called Sunday Sings. Onstage, I came in first with a book and sat and opened it as if I were opening the pages from which the group emerged.

"One performance, and then it was gone. It was the final performance of my dance company and my final performance as a dancer. I felt, at this time, that I did not want to dance anymore. I could still move very well, but I felt distressed when I saw people who I felt were pushing it beyond the time that they should have retired from the stage. I didn't think it was right for the public to see a wrong image of dance. I had gotten wonderful reviews, but little happened in the way of financial support."

May ended the summer in a workshop at University of California at Berkeley, July 5–26, 1961.

"Looking back at the activity of the 1950s, I don't know how I would have survived without the support of Ray and Gert."

39. May, teaching and rehearsing in London at The Place, 1959.

In 1961, Green was invited to the White House, along with a group of prominent composers and their wives, as guests of President and Mrs. Kennedy for a visit that included a concert by Pablo Casals.

The Greens were still their own team of creators, bookers, and press people without outside help or receiving the grants they deserved. "We just were too busy to stop and notice. And most of all, we wanted to decide for ourselves what to stage next, without any commitment to a financial source."

By 1961, May's accumulation of daily teaching, master classes, lecture/demonstrations, and dance works resulted in the workshop course, May O'Donnell Dance Technique and May O'Donnell Dance Patterns (combinations). It was, and still is, taught in colleges in America as well as in foreign countries.

In 1962, May created *Dance Scherzos* for her company to Green's music. That same year, Gert and May taught at the High School for the Performing Arts (1962–71) in New York City, where Rachel Yocum was chairman of the dance division. May at first resisted teaching in a school where her independence would be restricted and where the students would not have had the same early training. But, by continuing her company, she was able to balance teaching in a public school and creating works for them, as well as for her own company. Yocum, recognizing May's worth, placed no restrictions on her.

May and Gertrude Shurr taught at the high school with resounding success in producing professional dancers. They are listed here in order of their graduation dates: Daniel Lewis, Laura Dean, John Parks, Dennis Wayne, Gary Chryst, Dennis Diamond, Hector Mercado, Risa Steinberg, Jacquelyn Buglisi, Matthew Diamond, Mari Kjiwara, Keith Lee, and Susan McLain.

"I also taught at Mills College on Fifth Avenue at the same time. Some of my high school students got the experience of dancing in my company. The school classes were a different kind of creative challenge. It was tiring. Although I kept losing people to better-paying jobs and New York seasons with less touring, the challenge of making a new group look good on stage still fascinated me. So Gert and I kept on going.

"Years later, after a concert at Brooklyn College in 1978, some ladies asked me where I had been all this time. I said that I had been working on my Social Security. Gert nearly fainted at that remark, but it was true as well as funny."

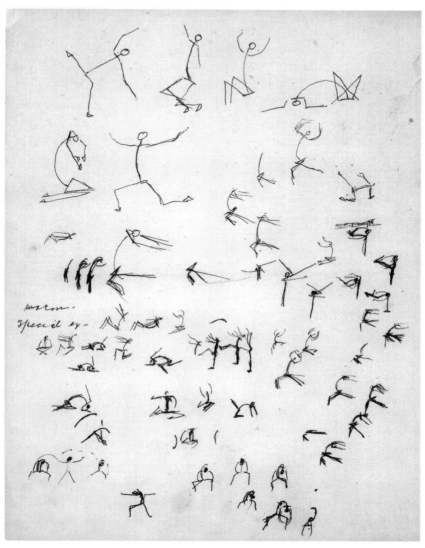

40. May's notation, 1960s.

41. May demonstrating exercises for her class, 1960s.

However, the teaching was rewarding, and those high school classes produced professionals such as Ben Vereen, Dudley Williams, and others. May could not remember the names of the small works she created for the yearly performances of the students.

Moving from studio space to studio space was, and still is, part of every dance group's New York experience—the never-ending search for a permanent and affordable commercial space. Beginning in 1944, Gert and May had their studio on University Place; they then moved to Fifty-sixth Street; and in the 1950s they found a place at 66 Fifth Avenue. It was a floor, though, and more than they could afford. The classes at Mills were held in the school gym as part of the gym program.

"In the Fifty-sixth Street studio, Ballet Theatre (now American Ballet Theatre) had its offices at the front of the building and we occupied the back. We had to share the bathrooms and became acquainted with each other in a strange kind of way! When the building was sold, we moved to the Fifth Avenue location, where we stayed until the early 1970s."

In 1972, a letter arrived stating that Mills College, like so many other organizations during the recession of the 1970s, had collapsed. Part of the income for the rent had disappeared. However, Gert and May found a space in a building being torn down where they were permitted to stay without fee until they could find another studio.

Then May got an invitation to teach in England at Robin Howard's London Contemporary Dance Theatre (founded in 1967). One of Martha Graham's former dancers, Robert Cohan, was the artistic director, and Jane Dudley, also from the Graham company, taught and staged works there. The school had an affiliated performing company, London Contemporary Dance Theatre, founded, with the school, in 1967. Cohan and Dudley wanted May to come to London to teach. May, while not interested in leaving to teach permanently, suggested she come to stage a work instead. In London, she staged her work *Dance Energies* and taught her technique. There were numerous performances of the work in England and the Continent, as well as during a tour of South America. The *Arts Guardian* (London) commented: "If there is an aristocracy of modern dance, then May O'Donnell belongs to it."

"The English company did my work very well, and it was well received. They had apparently had not done much larger movements in their dances, since Cohan had come from the Graham company and their works were more on the dramatic side. They seemed happy to move in a new way."

May returned to London to teach a two-week course in her technique in 1974 and again in 1976. While she was in London, Bethsabee de Rothschild, one of Martha's supporters who knew May, paid May a visit to ask if she would come to Israel. De Rothschild had settled in Israel in 1958 and there founded the Batsheva Dance Company (1964) in Tel Aviv and the Bat-Dor Studios of Dance and the Bat-Dor Company (1967).

"I was flattered, but it would mean spending a great deal of time away from my own school."

Just before May left for England, she and Gert had found a studio in a condominium that was being renovated. Since it was on the ground floor, descending dirt affected Gert's breathing. So they moved again, this time to Sixteenth Street, where they put in a new floor and once again got settled.

Eleven **The 1970s**

Although May had decided to end her performing career, her choreographic career continued to keep her busy.

"Just the year before the London trip [1971], Ramon Segara, who had been a student of mine at the high school, called me as a member of the Ailey company and asked me about reproducing *Suspension*. I revised the work to include two boys, Ramon and Dudley Williams, who was also a pupil of mine. Before, I had used only five girls. It was a new experience. I had two weeks to teach the work and an assistant to help me. I was concerned because it was a short time to put it together, and it's the kind of piece that dancers have to grow into. It's an inner piece, and the dancers have to bring a dimension to it that can only come out through a long experience. Otherwise, it can look like a line drawing instead of a finished work."

The Ailey company performed the work in New York and at the opening performance of the Kennedy Center in Washington, D.C. (October 1971) and on tour.

Because of the Ailey appearances in Houston (November 10) at Jones Hall, May received a grant to stage the work for the Houston Ballet. The Houston Ballet also took *Suspension* on tour.

As a result of the activity in London and Houston, May was asked to go to Oakland, California, where two former members of her company, Frank Shawl and Victor Anderson, had their own company and school. For them, she staged *Suspension, Dance Energies,* and *Dance Sonata.*

Because of all this activity, her students in New York wanted to learn her works as well. The dance company was reborn, and the programs were performed in the studio at Sixteenth Street on weekends. Rothschild and Jeannette Ordman, co-founder of Bat-Dor and director of its school, stopped by to see the concerts.

"Then, out of the blue, as it usually happens, the lease was up and the building was being co-oped. That was just too much. I had to go back to Berkeley to do a second piece, and there wasn't much time to look around.

"Gert retired because of her trouble breathing and went to live in Logan, Utah, and to winter in Tucson. I found a place on the tenth floor at Seventeenth Street, a big factory space with a hardwood floor. Because we didn't have to put down a new floor, only sand it, we stayed. I created *Pursuit of Happiness* (1977) there, and it seemed that our pursuit of happiness was always in finding a place to work. *Pursuit* was fun, and I used big band music of the 1930s and 1940s. The group performed it at the Delacorte Theater in Central Park two years after we had performed *Suspension* (1975) at the park.

"But again, the studio space was not ideal. The elevator would frequently get stuck, especially during the weekend performances.

"By the end of the year, a notice came that we had to move. In the meantime, I had to do some concerts at Brooklyn College in their dance series. We rented Paul Sanasardo's studio each day from 2:00 p.m. to 6:00 or 7:00 p.m. to rehearse for the series. We realized that we should have to either buy a place, if we were going to stay in dance, or look around once more. We found a place on Eighteenth Street between Fifth and Sixth Avenues, and again, it was on the tenth floor. Finally, in 1973, the May O'Donnell Modern Dance Center was established, with Ray as executive director. We purchased two floors of a loft building at 439 Lafayette Street."

From 1963 to 1970, Green took a sabbatical from composing as he applied hammer and nail, pioneer style, to his "inadvertently" acquired five old townhouses on East Seventh Street between Avenues C and D in Manhattan's Lower East Side. The purchase sustained the Greens and their O'Donnell-Green Music and Dance Foundation in their later years. Ray sold two, gave away two, and kept the three-story house, in which they remained.

"Before the renovation," May remembered, "the houses looked as if they were in a Charles Adams cartoon. They were dirty, cobwebbed, dingy, and dank. Ray renovated all of them as he took his time off. I don't know why he spent this time renovating the buildings except that it was almost another creative process for him and it involved our neighbors and helping others find a home. We both had an idea of sharing beyond our own lives. The neighborhood was dreadful, full of drug dealers and dangerous people, but somehow we who lived on this street got together and made it a decent place to live."

42. London Contemporary Dance Company in the pas de deux from May's *Dance Energies,* 1972.

Despite all the moving and teaching, by the end of the 1970s, May had found time to create *Pursuit of Happiness* (1977, Green), *Vibrations* (1978, Green), *In Praise of Chopin* (1979, to music of Frederic Chopin), and *Sonata in B-flat* (Green) the same year. May had lost dancers to paid rehearsals and performances in other companies.

"I constantly had to start over again with new groups that challenged my imagination. They wanted to look good, and they knew that I wanted them to look good."

The new O'Donnell Concert Dance Company, Inc., now established as a charitable nonprofit company, gave a total of nine studio performances of repertory works at the May O'Donnell Modern Dance Center. There were also performances at the College of White Plains in New York in 1975 and at the New York Dance Festival at the Delacorte Theater in Central Park. On June 13, 1976, the group gave its first paid performance, sponsored by the Rockaway Music and Arts Council, Inc. The National Endowment for the Arts granted

43. *Dance Energies*, London, 1972–73; opening section, London Contemporary Dance Company, Robert North, Noemi Lapzeson on box.

a travel stipend in 1976, which resulted in two high school performances at Long Beach Channel and in Rockaway, New York, both in 1976.

The spring concert series at May's studio in 1977 included the premiere of *Pursuit of Happiness.* Its first public performance was at the McKenna Theater at the State University of New York, New Paltz. That same year, the company performed at the Ted Shawn Theater at Jacob's Pillow. Other performances were held in and out of New York—at Pace College in White Plains, the College of Staten Island, and the Clark Center Dance Festival at the Mall at Forty-second Street between Fifth and Sixth Avenues.

In 1977, the National Endowment for the Arts provided a grant for *Vibrations* as a twelve-section work. It was set to Green's *Twelve Inventions for Piano Solo* and premiered at Gershwin Hall, Brooklyn Center for the Performing Arts at Brooklyn College, in January 1978. The company gave the world premiere of *Vibrations* at the Brooklyn Center for the Performing Arts, Brooklyn College, January 13–15, 1978. Adelphi College, Women's Exchange Theater,

Queensboro Community College, Philadelphia's YMCA, Alfred University, and the Wayne "Y" in northern New Jersey were added to the list of performance sites.

The Woodstock Playhouse in Woodstock, New York, included May's dance series of lecture demonstrations and practical information on pursuing a career in modern dance, as did the Brooklyn Center for Performing Arts at Brooklyn College, January 13–15, 1978.

The big band music of *Pursuit of Happiness* was the accompaniment at the Dance Umbrella series at the Entermedia Theater, in New York, on February 22, 25, and 26 and on November 8, 10, 11, and 12, 1977. The company appeared annually at the Woodstock Playhouse from 1978 to 1983.

The "discovery" of O'Donnell was made by *New York Times* critic Anna Kisselgoff, on February 24, 1978, at the Entermedia Theater performance: "What

44. Jacob's Pillow, 1977; *left to right*: Norman Walker, Gertrude Shurr, Ray Green, May O'Donnell.

45. May with her company at Brooklyn College, 1978; *in lifts*: Alice Gill, Regina Larkin, Dale Andree, Hazel Kandall, Donna Tchapraste; *boys*: David Cristel, Thomas Bain, Frederick McKitrick, Dale Orrin, Mark Maznio; *left of seated May*, Leslie Innis; *to her right*, Patricia Payne.

can one say, when the discovery of the dance season turns out to be a chore-ographer in her 70s with an outstanding young company in a superb pro-gram. All one can say is that no one interested in modern dance or beautiful dancing in general, can afford to miss the May O'Donnell Dance Company." In 1980, after a March 30 performance at the Riverside Church, Kisselgoff would write in the *New York Times*: "In the 1940s May O'Donnell was way ahead of her time in experimentation with dissociated movements."

"The company," wrote Clive Barnes in the *New York Post* in 1978, "is a knock-out. Her dancers are delightful, exquisitely and athletically trained and her choreography, some of it from her past, and some of it new, is extraordi-narily interesting."

The hectic barnstorming, reminiscent of the 1950s, continued: On May 13, 1979, Bennington College staged *Dance Energies, Suspension*, and *Pursuit of Happiness* at a celebration for the "Bennington College Pioneers," the fiftieth anniversary of the school to which May, as a former member of the Graham company and assistant to Louis Horst, and Ray, as composer of *American Document,* were invited. The Woodstock Playhouse engaged the company for a May 19 performance.

Other performances in 1979 included Queensboro Community College in New York on April 21, and a "Salute to Women," Arts Council, YWHA in Englewood, northern New Jersey, on May 5.

Although her recognition as a choreographer came late in her life, and her talent seemed to surprise and stun critics, May explained why she had continued:

"As a dancer, there is at least the possibility for a healthy life, a happy life, and a life of service and contribution. You're bound to be tested by the fates and conditions. And you have to try the best you can to somehow transpose yourself, to transcend that struggle. It's not easy, but we as dancers, I think have a better chance to try.

"The whole thing started when I first saw dance as a child and began wanting it very much. Then the search began. The journey is through a labyrinth, but there is a door and a key. But you have to recognize it and know what to hang onto. It may not always be the way you think that door should open or where you think it should be. But you hang onto the thread, you hang onto your life. Your strength is in a sense of mission, and your dedication to dance."

Frank Shawl, along with co-founder Victor Anderson of the Shawl-Anderson Dance Center in California, has been active as teacher and performing dancer throughout the United States and Canada. He has been a choreographer in the Bay Area for more than forty-three years. He appeared in concert with the Charles Weidman Company and for more than seven years (1951–57) with the May O'Donnell Dance Company, becoming her assistant. Shawl has taught, directed, and performed in Amsterdam and throughout the Netherlands and been the recipient of numerous awards. He shares these memories of working with May:

"There I was, just seventeen years old, having passed the Roxy Theater audition as a tap dancer, and performing four-a-day shows, five on weekends. But I knew I needed more technical strength. A dancer in the company offered to take me to the Shurr-O'Donnell studio on the street behind Carnegie

Hall, just a short distance from the Roxy. I would race, in full make-up, with no time to take it off or put it on between shows, to Gertrude Shurr's class. The work was so difficult, challenging, wonderful, and intriguing that even without previous comparison, I knew it was a strong technique and it was where I belonged. Every muscle in my body ached. Shurr gave you strength, unmannered technique, flexibility, and power.

"Ultimately, after showing progress, I was passed on to May, in a class of professional dancers from Broadway shows, modern dance, and ballet companies. Her work was demanding, inspiring, and the level of accomplishment by the dancers in the class enthralled me. The level of acceptance, encouragement, and support from teachers and other students was extraordinary. It was an oasis in the competitive world of classes.

"In class, May was always delving into new material that kept building and eventually found its way into her choreography. She opened an awareness of the unlimited extent of movement. Intuitively, she knew what our abilities were before we did. She showed us what mentoring is all about: being a guiding light, forever there, forever available, steady, true and free from artifice.

"Our relationship continued for fifty-two years. She was always a source of inspiration."

Word concerning Martha still reached May's ears. In 1969, when Martha was seventy-four years old, Ron Protas, Martha's longtime associate, saw her through a bout of alcoholism (rumored to be her second) while he administrated the school and company. May reacted:

"We couldn't believe what Martha was getting into with this arrangement. Protas seemed to be able to raise funds, and I couldn't blame Martha for her association with him for that reason."

Later, from 2000 on, there were several legal disputes about Protas's ownership rights to her works. A federal judge removed his trademark from her name, declared some works in public domain, gave one to Protas and others to the Martha Graham Center for Contemporary Dance. Ray Green, mindful of copyright law through his experience in music, began a project that put ten of May's works in copyright in 1991. That entailed videotape documentation and a copyright seal from the Library of Congress. May's works can now be staged as she created them.

Twelve The 1980s and Recognition

The highlight of 1975 for Ray Green was the publication for the American Music Edition of the Ph.D. dissertation based upon interviews of Green by Sidney Vise: *Ray Green, His Life and Stylistic Elements of His Music from 1935 to 1962*. It was published by the University of Missouri at Kansas City. A synthesizer would now enter into his scoring for May's *There Is a Time for Innocence* (1983) and *Powers of Ten* (1984).

Spring of 1980 found the May O'Donnell Dance Company at the Boston Conservatory of Music (April 18–20); and at the Riverside Dance Festival in New York the same month, with reappearances in 1981 and 1982 to follow. May 23 found the company at the Woodstock Playhouse with the premiere of *Homage to Shiva*, to traditional music of India. The summer included a month-long teaching workshop with May, as master teacher, and members of her company at Bennington College, ending with a concert on July 26. October was a busy month, beginning with the Friends of the Bayshore-Brightwaters Public Library in New York and the American College Dance Festival; the Emelin Theater in Mamaroneck, New York, had them perform on November 22. Appearances at the Arts Alliance in Philadelphia; the YMHA in Wayne, northern New Jersey; the Isabel Ferguson Performing Arts Center and the Ethel Walker School in Hartford, Connecticut (December 5) completed the year. May's frequent appearances in Woodstock earned her the following review by Jim Reed of the *Woodstock Times*: "Ease and naturalness address every complex pattern. She [O'Donnell] is never pretentious, never pedantic. Mind, heart, body and soul in her work are one."

Anna Kisselgoff of the *New York Times* continued her praise in 1980: "One can only marvel at the quality she has brought out in her dancers. They are instantly recognizable by the extraordinary combination of clarity and energy in their dancing. They move with an exceptional cleanness that is totally striking."

In 1981, May met a new challenge—television. CBS-Cable TV in Nashville featured May in an hour-long program including her *Dance Energies* and interviews with former students Robert Joffrey, Cora Cohan, Dudley Williams, and Gerald Arpino as well as Gertrude Shurr. Now the nation knew of May's work.

Touring continued as the company appeared April 4 at the Theater in the Park, Queens, New York. The Center for Modern Dance Education in Hackensack, New Jersey, invited the company to appear on May 16. June 10–14 found the company at the Newman/New York Public Shakespeare Festival, with the premiere of *Three Nocturnes and a Quartet* on June 12. The company appeared at the Woodstock Playhouse on July 27, and the American Dance Festival in Durham, North Carolina, brought the company out for a July 30 performance. The group appeared at the East Hampton Dance Festival (August 3–8), and at the Riverside Dance Festival (October 24–25). For the fiftieth anniversary of the Riverside Church (1981), Green created *Fanfare and Devotion*; *Three Nocturnes and a Quartet* was also performed.

> Joe Papp [producer of the Shakespeare Festival] has a nose for winners and presenting May O'Donnell at the Public Theater is right in line.
> —Barton Wimble, *New York Daily News,* 1981

> O'Donnell Dance Is a Happy Occasion
> —headline, *New York Post,* Don McDonagh, 1981.

On June 4, 1982, the company was once again invited to the John Drew Theater, Guild Hall, in East Hampton and to the Woodstock Playhouse on June 11. The Dance Theater Lab at Purchase, New York, invited the company on June 26, and the Lincoln Center Out-of-Doors series saw the company on August 14.

The company also performed that year for the Benefit for Inner City Ensemble in Secaucus, New Jersey; for the Dance Consortium at Northside High School in Atlanta; and at the Dellora A. Norris Cultural Arts Center, St. Charles, Illinois (November 6).

"It was there," May remembered, "in the concerts sponsored by the federal government in places that had never or seldom seen dance, such as in the

South, that we had our most gratifying experiences. Just the idea of bringing dance to the underprivileged makes all the difficulties seem unimportant. I felt that we were doing something worthwhile. Ray and I were givers, not in any moral or religious sense, but probably for our own sense of self-worth. When I think of just the example of the houses we gave away—they could have made us millionaires had we not done so. What reward, except money, would that have given us?"

At the Lincoln Center Out-of-Doors series sponsored by Exxon, Ben Vereen, one of May's students and company members, was now a famous performer. He gave a surprise introduction that delighted an audience of over six thousand for May's company performance.

That same year, the company appeared at the Waterman Theater in Oswego, New York, on April 16. Finally, a major theater series included May's company at the Joyce Theater in New York City, April 22–27, with Ben Vereen in the world premiere of *Echoes of a Lost Land* (Green). The Woodstock yearly appearance was on August 8, and a "Celebrate Brooklyn," fete on August 10 ended the month.

In 1983, the O'Donnell Dance Company and May were honored on two commercial programs—"Prime of Your Life," a network TV show, and *Woman of the Week.* That year, when the company appeared at the Joyce Theater with guest artist Ben Vereen, an hour-long feature of the work of May and Ray Green was filmed for the "Dance Master Series." Produced by Joseph Krakora, executive producer of the series and presidential advisor for the arts and humanities, the program was aired in 1984.

Life is a song and dance for this couple.
—Winnie Bonelli, *The Dispatch,* 1983.

The company performed in Brooklyn Park (June 30); Woodstock (August 8); in Ithaca (February 24), and once more at the Joyce Theater (March 22–27). Along with *Innocence* (from 1983), May prepared two new works for the 1984 season at the Joyce (May 15–20): *Powers of Ten,* to Green's solo synthesizer, and *Holiday for Four and Friends,* set to Green's *Chamber Quartet.*

In 1985, *Suspension* traveled to Holland and was staged and performed at the State Theater in Amsterdam by Dans/Kern, under the artistic directorship of Adriaan Kans, in 1985 and 1986.

The O'Donnell group performed for the Performing Arts Committee, Gettysburg College, Pennsylvania, on January 14. On January 26, there was a performance of Green's *Holiday for Four* at the Midtown YM-YWHA at a "Meet the Composer" symposium. It was under the auspices of the Yorktown Association for Performing Arts, Yorktown Heights, New York.

The two floors of the loft building at Lafayette Street for the May O'Donnell Dance Company and the May O'Donnell Modern Dance Center were sold in 1985. In that same year, the Greens launched a video project to record May's dance technique for use in colleges, universities, dance schools, and studios. Her technique has been taught at Adelphi University, Oberlin College, Dowling College, Westchester State College, Laban Centre in London, Dans/Kern in Amsterdam, in Italy and Switzerland, and at private studios in Taiwan. Her technique has been miraculously incorporated into the training of Cleveland's Dancing Wheels, a company for disabled and nondisabled dancers.

Woodstock Playhouse once again welcomed the company on June 23, 1986, performing a revised version of its *Holiday for Four*. Dance Space, in April 1987, introduced *Polka Sonatina*, while 1988 had a week (June 14–19) of invitational performances in celebration of the fiftieth anniversary of May and Ray Green's unprecedented creative collaboration and in celebration of their fiftieth wedding anniversary. The week of performances in New York included *Powers of Ten, Suspension, Three Nocturnes and a Quartet, Etudes and Scherzos*, one to six, all to the music by Green except for the *Nocturnes* by Chopin. The week of June 14–19 at the Classical Stage Company Repertory Theater was enhanced with a world premiere of *Etudes and Scherzos* to Ray's music for drum machine and percussion. It was the last performance of the company. In 1989, the Oakland Ballet in California performed *Pursuit of Happiness* (September 15–17) and for three years on tour.

There was one more premiere for the Greens, *Praeludium* (1993).

Ray Green's piano gala took place at Weill Recital Hall in Carnegie Hall, with three prize-winning pianists, Paul Komen (Amsterdam), Emily White (Miami), and Alan Mandel (Washington, D.C) performing works by Chopin and Green's *Sonata in C, Sonata in D,* and *Sonata in G*. The event was sponsored by the Chopin Foundation Council of Greater New York with support from the Netherlands-American Foundation. Again in 1990, prize-winning pianists David Beuchner and Emily White performed Green's works at

Carnegie's Weill Recital Hall. In 1991, another performance was held in the same hall with first-prize winners in the Frianna Auerbach International Competition of the Piano Teachers Congress of New York; and their not-for-profit Music and Dance Foundation sponsored the 1992 concert at the same hall with pianist Gary Steigerwalt and Emily White. In 1995, the Shanghai Philharmonic Symphony Orchestra performed Green's *American Sonatinas for Symphony Orchestra* and *Concerto in D for Piano and Orchestra,* conducted by Cao Peng with Albert Lotto, pianist. The concert was held in 1995 at Shanghai Concert Hall, China. "I guess we'll have to fly there," said May, a lifetime nonflier, admitted to Ray. Both Greens were present at the performance.

Thirteen O'Donnell Describes Her Technique

From 1938 to 1985, O'Donnell developed and taught her Dance Technique and Dance Patterns.

Teaching Technique

"I saw Doris Humphrey's work and liked it very much. It was *real* dance and had a lot of movement. Later, I had a little connection with her, a compliment, that meant a great deal to me. Her work was lyrical. I think Doris would have been an easier person for me to work with, more in tune with my natural self. But Martha forced me to think and move in a way that sometimes was not too natural for me. But it became part of my own movement experience, and I used it in my own way, if one can say that. I'm sure that I would have enjoyed working with Doris very much, but it just happened that I heard of Martha rather than Doris. Hanya Holm's work was in another form of dance that I saw and admired.

"When I first began to choreograph, I would go into the studio alone and start to explore. An inner pulse or rhythm emerged within my body. All outside influences were erased, and I would find a point at which I refreshed myself. I sought an inner place of balance, equilibrium, and order that would open channels of communication for my physical, intellectual, and emotional centers. At that point, my whole being came together in balance and harmony. My entire life has been a walk along that same creative path seeking balance and harmony.

"In teaching, once you develop a dancer to an advanced point, he or she wants to show it off. They want to exhibit their high jumps or turns because that's what they do best. But that's not dance. The public thinks it is, and so do a lot of dancers.

"Most of the people who come to class are not going to be dancers, but putting themselves in movement means a great deal to them. During the class, there's a concentration and purity. They give themselves to the learning and to the experience of moving. It awakens a spiritual need inside them, a need we all have beyond the material needs of living. When they release their spirit, their entire being becomes involved in what they're doing. They become different people, at least for the moment.

"I never thought of developing a syllabus when I choreographed or taught. There are certain principles that all of us must know: positions on the floor or standing, balance on one leg, the contraction-and-release principle, and the use of the arms. My range of motion started out small, at first, but developed when my dancers became more technically proficient. For instance, Bob Joffrey and Gerald Arpino in my company came from good ballet training by Mary Jane Wells in Seattle and were able to move more expansively. I did a lot of experimenting with the members of my company. With Joffrey and Arpino, despite their ballet technique, there was a lot that had to be worked out to suit the idea of whatever dance I was choreographing. I could build upon the talents of my dancers, unlike Martha, who created a role and then created movements to express the motivations and actions of that character."

Principles of O'Donnell's Technique

"My class would start as a warm-up on the floor in what I called key positions. I had a sequence that developed neuromuscular awareness. Along with warming up the body, stretching and strengthening exercises were included. I liked to do these warm-up exercises, the essential vocabulary and positions, in a sequence, not only to strengthen the back and entire body but also to stretch the skeleton.

"I did centering work to get students to hold their bodies properly. It seems like such a simple thing, but students have all kinds of natural misalignments.

"In teaching the contraction-and-release principle, I would tell the student to think of the spine as pulling under, with the image of the torso holding the shape of a barrel, a curve from the crown of the head to the end of the tail-bone. Then, in the release, the image is the rolling away of the barrel as the spine lengthens into a vertical position, a terrific stretch.

"The contraction-and-release principle can be incorporated into a variety of positions—standing, sitting, on the knees, balancing on one leg, and in other positions.

"Positions and movements indicate emotional states, such as the singing and jaunty movement of happiness or the heaviness of sadness. Dancers must become aware of these emotional states, as actors are aware of how these states react upon the observer. Eventually, they learn that if they use the body in a certain way, they're going to get a certain reaction. Emotions are stirred through the movement. It's the artist that has to do that for an audience. It's exciting and a wonderful adventure when you do something that can transpose the audience out of the mundane and routine.

"Most students are not aware of the shift of weight. Therefore, I developed a sequence of movement patterns on the floor, as well as in a standing position, to develop their awareness of the shifting of the weight from one position to another with the greatest ease, efficiency, and safety. Most students look a little surprised when you talk about shifting the weight. They think in terms of a walking pattern. In changing positions, the student must be aware of first *getting to the base*, the *control center*, to achieve the new position.

"Another aspect of my teaching was to make students aware of muscles that support the skeleton. Take away muscles and the skeleton would collapse. I also tried to create an awareness in the student of *inner muscles* and organs. These shape the exterior skin as if they were sculptor's clay. Depth and dimension are created.

"So many students, when they look at themselves in the mirror, think of dance as a position or a line. If they're not aware that line is motivated by the use of inner muscles and organs, they are only aware of the skin's surface, and have no sense of how to get into the muscles to produce a line. So it must be understood that the support of the skeleton is in the use of the inner muscles and ligaments.

"If the student's *spine* is curved in the lower back, as in a sway-back condition, for instance, until that spine is stretched through the pelvis to lengthen the back, the curve will remain until the condition is remedied.

"When the student feels the contribution of the inner muscles, they discover a depth and dimension in movement that is not only on the surface as a pose or a position. The reference point is the floor, the point of support where all movements are initiated.

"In standing, as well, I like to get the student to experience how it feels to hold the body through correct placement. And when they start to move, to be able to shift weight and still keep that strong placement. In jumps, correct placement works like a coiled spring that is pressed down carefully and released as elevation.

"Balance intrigued me. Early on, I was fascinated by mobiles and their mechanics. Like mobiles, there is a *balancing point* in the core of the body. The spine is that core. The concept is that, even in the most intricate positions, we may assume that each member of the whole could have an individual life as in a mobile. The head could go in one direction or position, the arms in another, the legs in still another, yet wholeness is retained. In my work *Suspension*, each dancer holds his own magnetic field as part of the whole in their eternal pattern, without colliding with another pattern. It is a kind of law of nature. The reaction is sometimes that of loneliness, but that is the independence and the interdependence of the piece to all the parts as a whole.

"As in dance, a good relationship between our three centers—physical, intellectual, and emotional—makes us much happier and more realistic as human beings. We have to explore and discover our possibilities, rather than just stay the way we are. There is always resistance, first from our own physical sluggishness and the complacency in which we might find ourselves. We might worry about what society or our family might think about our taking our chances and putting ourselves into a situation that might seem alarming. But when I think of our pioneers and the chances they took as they started out to trek across to the unknown West, it was all necessary to make their great discoveries.

"I like to do extensions, jumps, and combinations of these. I never talked very much about any of these things as technique. I just worked with them.

"Breath has a force to bring life into your face and body. Through breath, the body can be taken into a magical realm, into a transcendent state. I saw students with such deadpan faces. I said, 'Think of being an opera singer—use your ears, your eyes, your mouth, and use the sound of breathing. It should be as if you're singing when you dance.' I encouraged them to *lift* into movements, as if they were a conductor giving beats to music."

The Power of Movement

"So many young people are matter-of-fact about what they do. It may be their idea of dancing. It may be the times. Times were grim in the 1930s when we were fighting the big pioneer battle of new dance. But before that, when you think of Isadora Duncan, for instance, you think of a glorious kind of fullness of movement, a lift of the body. Students are very conscious about lifting their legs, but little thought is given to lifting their body or their spirit. Physically, as a matter of safety, the body has to lift off the knees in descending or ascending to them. The entire body supports the movement and the knees are not slammed into the floor.

"I liked to talk as I taught and to sing the movements with accents and phrasing. I used to sing or hum when I danced, although I can't sing! It was just kind of a rhythm, a kind of sound that opened the face with energy, and got the body and legs going. It is something each student has to discover. It cannot be taught. Religious groups know the power of sound, and I find it more convincing than using a drum.

"The human body is a miracle. I love to see people move beautifully. When a movement didn't look good, I changed it.

"I got my students off the floor sooner than was done in Martha's classes. I wanted them to move. Gert [Shurr] was precise and strict in teaching the basics and developing muscular strength. By the time they got to my classes, we had gotten them to move lyrically and musically and to cover space.

"Musically, although Ray wrote atonal music in some cases, odd counts, no bars or melody to hang onto, there seemed to be no trouble for me in finding his work as a collaboration to what I was doing. Rarely, I would ask for greater length, a longer passage, for instance. We seemed to work together in the spirit of the piece instead of becoming involved in the craft of making a dance. There were no rules. At times, I would get an idea inspired by a dancer who had a particular quality, and I would use that quality as the motive for a work.

"I didn't get always get the best dancers to work with—no choreographer does all the time—but that's the challenge, making people look good and giving them something to express in their movements beyond their physical limitations. The dancers were loyal to me for that reason. I didn't have a fixed idea that a dancer had to fit into my choreographic ideas or become disregarded. Everyone, if they were enthusiastic and had something to offer me became part of a sweet exchange between us. They gained in self-esteem and were grateful and willing to try new things.

"It's a funny thing about movement, why some people can move and some cannot. For some, physical movement is a great release; for others, inhibiting. How dancers move is not entirely mental or the result of the training process, but somewhat dependent upon the construction and mechanics of the body. Short, compact people seem to move quickly; the taller ones cover more space but need more time to do so. A natural bounce in jumps is there in the body, or it isn't. If a dancer, as a youngster, didn't play games that made them move nor engaged in sports, no matter how deep their desire, dance will take more time."

Inspiration

"Depending upon the subject, I would describe my work as being more lyrical than dramatic. Since I came from the West, my dances were open, like a range, or the mountains in my vision. I wanted everything to move over space and look free . . . if a dance can be explained.

"The environment of dance is always affirmative. It's so easy to be negative when most of the world is negative. Everything wants to pull you back into that and you have to transcend. You're bound to be tested by the fates and conditions, but conditions can be turned around. We live in such freedom in so many ways, there is always the possibility of finding a new way to express ourselves.

"There is a kind of liberty in dance that doesn't restrict, the way religion does, for instance. The creative spirit in dance is wide, endless, always there. For the student, all the body requirements pile up and seem to obscure the spirit. But you can call upon spirit for inspiration at any time, any place, at any age.

"I can still remember how often my mother and I would go to Cliff House in San Francisco, down to the beach and take our shoes off and walk around.

The sun was so large, and watching it set made us full of wonder. The colors were beautiful, and the movement so steady and slow. As often as we saw it, it was still majestic and inspiring each time.

"Ray and I traveled often across the country, and we let nature come into our lives instead of rushing to get to our destination. The valleys and canyons, the rhythm of the wind, the waterfalls, and especially the quietness, except for the migration of birds, or the echo of a train whistle, gave us spiritual refreshment. There was the smell of orange trees and the colors of green in leaves and grass. The Navahos colored sand to use in their traditional designs that are so precise and geometrical. It was a ritual they permitted us to watch.

"I feel that dancers today are very different from dancers of the past. Today, people don't go far enough in their training for modern dance. Contemporary choreography doesn't demand as much technically. Some dancers are better today, but most, not as good as in the 1950s, for instance. Anyone can learn to lift a foot, but what that movement insinuates is the thing that dance is all about. There's wonder in lifting an arm, for instance. No matter what the shape of a movement, if the dancer doesn't breathe life into it, it is nothing. Each must feel the *possibilities* in movement. And each must have enough control to forget technique. In the long run, the performer must be generous . . . at least, while they're on stage!"

Dudley Williams was in May O'Donnell's company in the 1950s, in Martha Graham's Contemporary Dance Company in the 1960s and is currently a performer and teacher in the Alvin Ailey American Dance Company. He commented:

"Although May gave master classes at the High School for the Performing Arts, Nancy Lang, one of her company members, was my original teacher. It was 1955, and I was graduated from the school in 1958.

"May taught us to lift in and up with the muscles beneath the ribs, the section of the body Isadora Duncan named the solar plexus. This is not contrary to the contraction-and-release principle, but part of the support system. I still teach that principle at the Ailey and Graham schools. You push your shoulders down and tighten up the pectoral muscles.

"Nancy took Eleo Pomare, Mabel Robinson, and me to May's studio. We were the most gifted black dancers in the school. Nancy introduced us to May along with Ramon Segara and Robert Powell. May took the five of us under

46. CBS-TV photo of May's *Pursuit of Happiness*, 1989; *left to right*: Lauren Phillips, Terry Howard, Barbara Allegro, David Christel, Alyce Bochette, Dale Orri, Nancy Lushington.

47. *Pursuit of Happiness*, 1989, CBS-TV photo; *left to right*: Nancy Lushington, Lauren Phillips, Alice Gill, Barbara Allegro, Alyce Bochette.

48. May and Ray, in Prospect Park, Brooklyn, 1980.

49. *Dance Energies,* 1980 version; *left to right:* Barbara Allegra, Nancy Lushington, and Alyce Bochette in a studio pose.

50. *Dance Energies,* restaged in 1980s; *left to right, standing:* Nancy Lushington, Alyce Bochette, David Christel, Alice Gill; *kneeling:* Sabatino Verlezza, Dale Orrin; *sitting, front row:* Lauren Phillips, Barbara Allegra; *sitting, back row:* Diane Sawyer, Terry Howard.

51. Ben Vereen, Alice Gill in May's *Homage to Shiva*, 1983.

52. David Christel in studio pose, 1980s.

53. (*Opposite, top*) David Christel and Alice Gill in *Homage to Shiva*, 1980s.
54. (*Opposite, bottom*) Alice Gill in *Dance Concerto* (1954), in a 1980 version.

her wing and was absolutely wonderful to us. She and Gertrude were like two mothers who taught, guided, and provided for us. If, for instance, one of us said, 'May, I don't have the carfare to go home,' she'd give it to us without hesitation or comment. If we hadn't eaten lunch, she would bring us cookies and tea. 'Come, eat, darling,' she would say, 'eat as much as you want and don't worry about it.'

"Class was at 4:30, and when the door to the studio was closed, we would wait outside and hear May making a sweeping noise like Zoom! Zoom! Zoom! We always wondered what was going on. Finally, we asked Gertrude, who said that May was choreographing or taking her own class. When May opened the door, she would be out of breath and her hair would be in her face. 'Ah, that was wonderful,' she'd say, then she would give us what she had just created. The studio had no mirrors. She was our mirror, and our accompaniment was her drum.

"Her company at that time included Robert Joffrey, Gerald Arpino, and Jonathan Watts, and I felt so fortunate to dance with those people. She was remarkable in creating movement for boys. Reckless abandonment I called it. In *Dance Energies* [1959], Bill Luther and I had a duo that was fantastic. The rhythms that May and Ray gave us were unforgettable. Years later, whenever Bill and I met, we talked about nothing else. The work's changes in tempo, legatos, dynamics, and push for more and more energy exhausted us. I still get goose bumps just thinking about it. It was exhilarating to do, satisfying and gave us a sense of accomplishment.

"Then there was *Dance Sonata #1* [1952], *Illuminations* [1956], and *Theme and Variations* [1945, revised] that we all were proud to do. I still teach what I can remember from *Legendary Forest* [1954], and the students are entranced with the change of accents in doing what is essentially little attitudes to the sides. While May performed those roles for Graham of great outer stillness and inner reaction, she gave us the opposite to do: sweeping steps slashing through space, bounding jumps, a constant succession of patterns. Martha's work was on the floor. May's work was in the air. Louis Horst used to say 'earth primitive, air primitive.' They each have their sovereignty.

"May was so musical and on occasion we had the treat of Ray Green playing various instruments for our class. The shape of the movements and the rhythms were totally clear. The sound of Ray's score, when we rehearsed to tape, became part of the movement, its sonority, its phrasing and dynamics were all part of the performance quality.

"Or course, because we often performed in college towns and were still youngsters, we took off, to May's consternation. She wanted to know where her family was at all times. As New Yorkers, the mountains and woods lured us, and when we found someone with a car, we rode off to drink and enjoy the summer. Nothing serious, but we never saw May angry; she was always patient. Gertrude would get angry with us, and we would giggle because she had a funny way of doing it.

"May, as Mother Bird, wanted us to see the world and go out of the nest. She knew that she would lose us to other jobs that were better-paying, but she wanted us to explore other possibilities.

"May was before her time in creating abstract works, while all the story ballets were going on. But May's work is enduring. I can still remember and teach her technique, and so can all or us who attended her classes or were in her company."

Fourteen **O'Donnell's Intermediate Class**

This class, transcribed from a videotape, was instructed by former O'Donnell company member and now teacher Nancy Lushington at Marymount College, New York City, in 2003. Read all exercises carefully before executing, and repeat all to left side.

I. Floor Warm-up

1. On counts 1 and 2, at a fairly moderate tempo: Sitting on the floor with straight legs, toes pointed, with rounded arms in lowered Second Position, fingers extended (not rounded), flex feet and contract with knees slightly bent as arms move to First Position at chest level. On counts 3 and 4: Release by rolling up to a straight back, lifting the muscles beneath the ribcage as the arms open to lowered Second Position, knees straight and feet pointed. Execute the exercise 4 times.

2. On counts 1 and 2, at the same tempo: Continuing with arms in Second Position, now at shoulder height, feet flexed, twist to the right in a contraction, knees bent slightly as left arm crosses in front of body toward right arm, head turns to the right. On counts 3 and 4: Release to arms in Second Position, head straight, feet pointed, knees straight. Repeat same exercise to the left, twisting torso and turning head to the left. Execute 4 times, twice each side.

3. On counts 1 and 2: Continuing in the same starting position, contract, knees slightly bent, feet flexed; raise arms in front slightly higher than shoulders with flexed wrists. On counts 3 and 4: Lower arms front to shoulder height and curve them slightly in lifted release, knees straight, feet pointed. Execute the exercise 4 times.

4. On the count of 1: With wrists and feet flexed, contract and twist torso to right, keeping arms in previous shoulder height position. On the count of 2: Release, remembering to lift under rib cage as the body returns to center on counts 3 and 4. Repeat exercise to left with a twist to the left and return. Arm positions remain the same. Repeat exercise 4 times. End series with arms slightly lowered in Second Position.

II. Head and Arm Circles

1. In 4 counts: Sitting cross-legged, wrists alongside knees, chin resting between collar bones, torso lifted, rotate head to right, back, left, and return to position of chin resting between collar bones. Repeat full head circle to left. Repeat right and left.
2. On counts 1 and 2: From same starting position of chin between collar bones, drop head with right ear on right shoulder, rotate head down and left in a half-circle. On counts 3 and 4: Repeat to left. Execute exercise right and left in half-circles.
3. Repeat in one-and-one-half circles. On count 1 and 2: Torso tilts to right, straight left arm to the side higher than shoulder level, in line with lowered straight right arm. Raise left knee slightly off floor still in the cross-legged position, head straight. Bend head and body down to right knee, using right hand as support to widen the circle; rotate head down, left and back switching to left hand on floor as support. On counts 3 and 4: Head continues to right and down as one circle and continues down and around to the left as a half-circle. Exercise ends in tilt to left, right arm raised matching left in one line, right knee slightly off floor as exercise continues with head making one-and-one-half circles, body ending opposite side in the tilt position. Execute exercise 4 times.
4. Exercise of head circles continues with deeper circles. On counts 1 and 2: Tilting to the left, fingertips on floor, right arm extended higher than shoulder height in one line with left arm, as above; left arm swoops down and around overhead as it meets right arm, which now continues the wide circle to the left. On counts 3 and 4: Right arm continues down and around, ending with fingertips on floor and body in tilt position to the right. Repeat to the left.

Support the swoops with fingertips on floor during down and back movements with each one-and-one-half circle to enlarge the circles. Execute 4 times, keeping movements continuous, smooth, and rhythmic. As an aid, remember that the left arm initiates the down swoop when the circle is to the left; right arm initiates the movement when circle is to the right.

III. Stretches on the Floor

During this long series, hips should be kept square throughout all exercises. The exercises begin in almost the same pattern, but end in a different pose to begin the next exercise.

All releases should be high, meaning lifted and beneath the rib cage. Keep in mind that an inhale of breath accompanies a lifted movement, and an exhale accompanies a lowering movement. This enables the lift in a release, for instance, to be supported by breath and a lowering movement to become supple, neutral, and ready for the next movement.

1. This set of exercises is executed at a fairly brisk tempo. In 4 counts, legs together straight forward, bend body forward to place hands on ankles. With a round back, pulse or lightly bounce forward with flexed feet 4 times in a contraction. Then, with a straight back, pulse in release with pointed feet. Repeat. Pulse forward once more with a round back, hands on ankles as above, then with a straight back and pointed feet as the arms reach forward at shoulder height during the pulses. Head remains in line with the spine throughout.

2. In 4 counts: With knees bent to the side and soles of the feet together, hands on ankles, pulse with a rounded back, 4 times in contraction. In 4 counts: Release and pulse 4 times with a straight back. Repeat exercise.

3. In 4 counts: Extend right leg on floor to side, foot pointed, arms in Second Position. Contract as torso leans and arms stretch forward, fingers flattened, and right foot flexes. Release as arms open slightly and torso is raised with pointed foot in 4 counts and arms move to Second Position. In 2 counts: twist torso to right as left arm meets right arm in First Position facing right. Torso leans to right knee in contraction, arms extended still

in First Position, right foot flexed, arms reaching forward, fingers flattened. On counts 3 and 4: Release and return to center position with left arm moving to Second Position, right foot pointed.

In the lean and contraction forward with flexed foot, arms should reach forward in First Position, fingers flattened. A high release is executed as arms open to Second Position. Repeat exercise to left.

Repeat exercise with torso twisting left as right arm moves to meet left arm in First Position. Lean forward in contraction over left knee, right foot flexed. Release on lifted torso and end in Fourth Position (left leg turned out, bent with outer side of knee on the floor, right leg extended in back turned in, knee on floor). Repeat entire exercise to the left ending in Fourth Position.

4. On counts 1 and 2: Remaining in Fourth Position, stretch the torso forward toward left front corner along floor as arms reach forward, back straight. On counts 3 and 4: Torso rises onto knees, as arms reach overhead and end in Second Position, elbows curved. (Hips face left front corner.)

5. On counts 1 and 2: Torso leans forward in contraction toward left knee, sitting in Fourth Position as in previous exercise, arms in lowered Second Position. On counts 3 and 4: Right arm swings down, rises to overhead, and returns by the same path around head and down to open right above shoulder height in release. Left hand-to-elbow on the floor supports the deep circle as torso leans back as far as possible with hips raised.

On counts 1 and 2: Sitting in Fourth Position, right arm swings down and overhead, returns along the same path, ending in Second Position with both arms curved, fingers downward, elbows slightly bent. On counts 3 and 4: Repeat the same exercise ending with a rise to the knees, arms in same ending position.

6. On counts 1 and 2: Torso lowers to sitting in Fourth Position, right arm swings down as torso leans front to floor, and arm circles to overhead, returns downward along the same path, and ends straight above shoulder height to the right. On counts 3 and 4: In 2 counts: As right arm reaches overhead position, left leg straightens on floor, hips raise as left arm in hand-to-elbow position on floor supports a lean backward. Left leg and right arm are now in one long line with hips raised. On counts 3 and 4:

Lower torso, and right arm swings front and down, around to Second Position as torso rises to Fourth Position facing left on knees. Repeat exercise
ending with torso up on knees. Swivel on left knee on floor ending right
knee bent, right toe resting and supporting on floor.

7. In 2 counts: Place right knee on floor in Fourth Position, swing right arm
down and around to overhead, straightening left leg as the torso rises, supported by left arm in hand-to-elbow position on floor. On counts 3 and 4:
Right arm swings down as torso sits in Fourth Position, ending with a
twist in the torso to the right, straight right leg off the floor at 45 degrees
front, both arms on floor behind torso supporting the right lifted leg.

8. Repeat the exercise ending with right leg as high as possible and both
arms reaching toward right foot with body supported on left knee.

9. Repeat the exercise ending with right leg raised and caught at the inside
heel by right hand on counts 3 and 4. Left hand is on the floor for support.

10. On counts 1 and 2: Continuing in the same position with right leg caught
at the inside heel by right hand, bend right knee in same position, and
raise left arm in curved position overhead. On counts 3 and 4: Torso, head,
and curved left arm lean toward right knee. In 4 counts: Right straightens
as torso leans slightly back, left arm remains curved. Repeat.

11. In 4 counts: Maintaining the same pose, swing left arm down in front of
torso to overhead curved position, with right knee slightly bent. Hold 4
counts with left arm curved slightly past overhead. Repeat.

Repeat with previous arm swings and hold in 2 counts. In a percussive
movement, end last swing on knees, arms curved and in lowered Second
Position, fingers downward, hips facing front left corner.

12. On counts 1 and 2: Lower torso to a sitting position, stretching arms to
corner front left. On counts 3 and 4: Rise on knees with arms overhead
ending in arms curved in a percussive (strong and accented) lowered Second Position, fingers downward, elbows bent.

13. Sit and repeat exercise over right knee, arms up and forward, and end on
knees with percussively placed curved arms.

14. Repeat exercise ending with right leg stretched back on floor, torso twisted
left and leaning to the floor, left knee bent, head to floor.

15. On counts 1 and 2: With both hands on floor for support, lift upper torso,
neck, and head stretched into an elongated long parallel to floor. On

counts 3 and 4: Right leg lifts from the floor in an arabesque. (This exercise is dubbed the "gargoyle.") On counts 3 and 4: Return to floor position as in previous exercise and rise again into gargoyle position.

16. Repeat twice lowering upper body to floor, extending right leg into arabesque position, forehead to floor, then ending with head and upper back raised and stretched, right leg slightly off floor in attitude (slightly bent knee) position back. Right leg returns to arabesque position as exercise is repeated.

17. On counts 1 and 2: Shifting to a "sit" Fourth Position with right knee on floor back and left knee on floor in front. On counts 3 and 4: Left arm circles overhead ending with both hands on floor to support both legs swiftly straightening out as torso rests on left hip. Head faces left in profile. Repeat.

18. Repeat exercise sitting in Fourth Position, circle left arm and end on left hip, legs straight, then raise right leg to à la seconde position (90 degrees). Head faces left in profile. Repeat exercise with same ending.

19. On counts 1 and 2: Sitting in Fourth Position, in left-to-right movement, circle left arm overhead. On counts 3 and 4: Right arm circles with both ending on hands and straight legs in a swift movement and lifted torso resting on left hip. Repeat twice ending left, then repeat ending on right hip with arms circling from right to left, ending with hands on floor and straight legs with right hip on floor.

Repeat entire section III, stretches on floor, to left side beginning with exercise 3, left leg extended.

IV. Floor Adagio

1. In a slower tempo, on counts 1 and 2: Sitting on floor in Second Position with arms out to sides, feet pointed, slowly and smoothly bend forward as arms reach forward at shoulder height and feet flex. On count 3 and 4: Return arms to Second Position at ankle level as torso and arms rise to upright Second Position, toes pointed. On counts 5 and 6: Turn torso to right as left arm meets right in First Position and torso slowly bends forward toward right flexed foot. Raise torso and return to upright position, arms in Second Position, toes pointed. On counts 1 and 2: Repeat bending

forward with arms reaching forward, feet flexed. Open arms to Second Position at ankles. Then raise torso with arms remaining in Second Position. On counts 3 and 4: Turn torso to left, right arm meets left and upper body bends toward left flexed foot. Torso rises and returns to Second Position, toes pointed.

2. On counts 1 and 2: With knees bent to sides on floor and sitting tailor or akimbo fashion, outer foot right in front of left bent knee, arms in Second Position, bend slowly and smoothly forward, as in the first exercise, reaching forward with arms at shoulder height. On counts 3 and 4: Torso lifts as arms move backward into lowered Second Position, fingers downward. Repeat forward stretch and lifted torso with arms stretched backward.

3. On counts 1 and 2: From Second Position, turn right, straighten right leg on floor, left leg is bent with inner knee on floor. Torso bends forward, hands on floor for support. On counts 3 and 4: Body slowly rises to stretched position, legs straighten, torso still facing right, head down. Repeat exercise to right side.

4. Using the same counts: repeat exercise bending forward and ending upright on left knee, right leg straight, hands on floor. Return to sitting position and repeat bending forward ending with rise with both legs straight as torso continues to bend forward, hands on floor for support and left leg straightens in back. Lower the torso with straight legs into a front split. Rise, using hands on floor and lower to split again.

5. On counts 1 and 2: In sitting position, right foot on floor in front of torso, left knee on floor, right arm reaches overhead in a large sweep and descends as torso turns left, both elbows on floor, head down. Then torso stretches upward. On counts 3 and 4: With head down in bend, stretch torso upward and end with left leg straightened, arms still on elbows but stretched out to accommodate straight left leg. Position is supported on right foot and hands.

6. On counts 1 and 2: In sitting position facing left with right foot still on floor, right arm reaches overhead left and around to right, swings back again in the same pattern—as left arm is on floor hand-to-elbow position—and ends with both arms straight and reaching to the right, in profile right. Head follows arm. Repeat, ending with both elbows bent.

7. From sitting position, two arms stretch left in slight lean backward, then back and right as movement ends right with same arm pattern: both arms bent at elbows. Repeat.

8. On counts 1 and 2: In same sitting position, right arm swings right, overhead, and back in full circle ending with torso leaning back supported by two straight arms, then lowering onto flat back. On counts 3 and 4: Torso rises, right arms swings in same overhead pattern, down around into flat back lean to floor and up to bent elbow position. Repeat.

Repeat section IV, floor adagio, to left beginning at exercise 2.

V. Center and Balances

1. On the count of 1: Standing upright, facing front with feet in First Position, arms alongside of body, palms facing in, raise the arms to chest level (First Position), hands slightly apart and to overhead on the count of 2; to the side at Second Position with palms up on the count of 3. Rotate and return to arms alongside torso on the count of 4, all in a continuous movement. The quality is light, soft, and smooth. Reverse in 4 counts.

2. On the count of 1: With feet in Second Position, raise right arm to First Position with head right following arm to Second Position, then left arm and head left. Arms then rise overhead on the count of 2; descend right arm and head, left arm and head, to Second Positions. Head ends in center. Repeat beginning with left arm and head movements. Repeat adding a high release (head back) when arms reach overhead. Head returns when arms are in Second Position.

3. On the count of 1: Feet in First Position, demi-plié as arms rise to Level One or First Position, then relevé to demi-pointe position (onto metatarsals, heels up) slowly on the count of 2 as arms rise overhead. Lower heels and demi-plié on the count of 3, as arms descend to Second Position and return to original position on the count of 4 with heels down. Reverse movement beginning in demi-plié with arms alongside, rise to demi-pointe on the count of 2 as the arms rise to the side and overhead. Lower heels and demi-plié as arms return to First Position (level 1) and alongside on counts 3 and 4. Repeat movement with high-release on descent of overhead movement. All movements are slow and continuous in 4 counts.

4. Repeat the above exercise with same arm movements beginning in demi-plié, followed by a rise to demi-pointe with arms overhead and adding a grand plié as arms descend to Second Position.

5. With right arm at chest level, left in Second Position, shift weight onto left leg as right assumes tendu position. Battement tendu (or brushes) side 7 times and return to First Position each time. Shift the body weight through a demi-plié in Second Position and reverse weight to right leg on the count of 8. Tendu (brushes) using the left leg to the side, left arm chest level, right arm to side, and do 7 brushes or battements tendus.

VI. Fourth Position Bounces

1. Facing front, with right leg in tendu back, demi-plié and maintain weight on left leg (Fourth Position). With left arm side, right arm at chest level, bounce 5 times pressing right heel down at each movement. Rise in tendu right leg back on a straight left leg and close into First Position, heels together. Reverse with right arm side and left at chest level.

2. Facing front right corner, or in croisée position, repeat 5 bounces with left leg in front tendu position, left arm to side, right at chest level, ending with heels together. Tendu the last movement slightly off the floor in order to close in First Position, heels together. Repeat in croisée (crossed in front of supporting leg) position to the left, changing arm positions, last tendu slightly off the floor to enable the heels to come together and close in First Position.

3. Facing front, bounce in Fourth Position front as in exercise above with right leg in tendu 5 times. (A bounce is simply the gentle lowering of the heel of the foot that is in tendu position.) End the exercise after the fifth bounce in passé, right foot to left knee. Close with heels together and repeat to the left ending with left foot at the right knee. Repeat exercise in croisée position right and left.

4. Repeat Fourth Position with right leg in tendu back for bounces and end counts 6, 7, and 8 with a passé (right foot to left knee) and développé front (unfold to straight right leg). Repeat to left ending with passé left and opening leg to front on 6, 7, and 8. End with heels together, First Position.

5. Repeat 5 bounces in croisée position using right leg in tendu front, and

ending in passé facing front and dévelopé to the right side. Repeat using left leg in tendu position. (All endings that change the starting position require a slight shifting movement by the heel of the supporting leg to make the transition smoothly.)

VII. Prances

Facing right, raise right knee front 3 times; step forward on half-point front on right, then left foot front in half-point, closing feet in parallel position, heels down. Repeat using left leg stepping backward and closing in parallel position front. Repeat 3 knee raises with side step to the right ending in parallel, then 3 left knee raises with step to the left ending in parallel position. Repeat pattern to the left side.

VIII. Center Adagio

Grand plié in First Position, heels together, arms rising overhead from Second Position. Rise to passé and dévelopé right tilting to left, arms in Second Position. Plié on left leg slightly and rotate body to the left moving supporting heel and ending in arabesque, right leg up, torso facing left; left leg remains in slight plié. The right arm moves overhead to front. Change positions through a deep plié in Second Position with arms swinging gently down and weight transferring to right leg remaining in plié as left leg moves into a high arabesque. Torso straightens as left leg ends in passé, arms overhead. Close with heels together and begin exercise to left side.

IX. Triplets and Variations

1. Starting at far corner of the studio facing left, do triplets crossing to opposite corner of the room. (Triplets begin with a step forward in plié on the accent count of 1; a step left and then right on half-pointe on counts 2 and 3. Repeat beginning with left foot.)
   Continue across the floor.
2. Return to starting point in triplets beginning on right leg with a full, swift

pivot turn to the right on count 3 on the right leg. Repeat beginning on left foot with pivot turn on left leg. Continue across the floor.

3. Add a pivot turn on count 2 of the triplet. Continue across the room. Return to starting point.

4. Repeat triplets adding a deep, sliding plié on the count of 1 and retain the turn on the count of 3. The opposite arm reaches forward on the count of 1. Return.

5. Add a deep croisée plié on right leg, with hips well forward on count 1 adding a striking, slashing right arm movement overhead in the plié movement. Counts 2 and 3 are plain walks. Repeat the slashing movement in plié movement to left, and alternate these triplets across the room. Repeat.

6. Add arms overhead with torso leaning back on count 1 of the forward movement; arms down leaning forward on next triplet and moving backward. Continue with opposite arm forward and pivot turn on 3, as in previous exercises and slashing movements on next set of triplets.

X. Jumps

1. In First Position, sauté (jump) 4 times in place, 4 times moving forward, ending on left foot. Hop on left foot as right leg pumps backward.

    Chassé back to original place, right facing upstage. Turn and chassé left facing downstage. Repeat.

2. Crossing the room and in a running motion, run on the right foot, then the left, and split leap onto the right foot on count 3 and descend on count 4. Repeat beginning with the left foot, right and split leap on the count of 3. Alternate feet in a continuous crossing to the other side of the space or studio.

Révérence

These movements vary but are basically a winding down of energy and breath and indicate reverence and appreciation for the teacher's contribution to the class. The group follows the teacher in the movements that are seldom the same in every class and consist of any number of slow, courteous bows or other movements such as upright stretches and ports de bras (arm movements). Applause for the teacher also signals the end of the class before it exits, unless the teacher waves it off.

Frank Shawl Describes O'Donnell's Technique

"Exercises from a class cannot describe May's specific artistic demands for the execution of her unique and distinctive technique.

"May's work requires the completion and extension of a line in every part of the body as it moves in space. By mentally focusing beyond the walls or ceiling of the studio, boundaries are eliminated. Incorporated into this process are dynamic changes of direction to be executed with crisp and clear command. The degree of energy required and the timing of all movements rests on the phrasing of her extraordinary musicality, frequently used in mixed meter and incorporating diverse qualities.

"The technique demands articulate feet and legs, developed through total muscular involvement and commitment to the movement; a wide-open upper back with a lifted sternum; an energized, lengthened spine rising from anchored hips even in floor movements; and the continuation of the spine through a long neck and seeming to continue beyond the top of the head.

"Total muscular engagement without a moment of settling or slackness is necessary during the execution of the contraction-and-release principle. Each shape is equally, viscerally engaged.

"Arms are kept simple and are used as an extension of the torso, especially the upper back. They float gently in a pure form even when used in opposition to the working leg.

"No less important is the attitude of the student. May wanted to see a pupil infused with youthful energy, alert with eagerness to master a movement through all its evolutions, an alive face and a willingness to commit to detailed and frequent repetition with a sense of adventure. She wanted to see the student's passion for movement and an individual spirit visible in the execution of that movement.

"Her goal was to give the dancer a technique not only as a set of tools but as a means to develop his or her inner person to become an artist with expressiveness and individuality. She also wanted to develop that student's talent into an artist with the capacity to resonate to the material within the material, to claim it and transmit it beyond the space of the stage.

"A commitment to May's work is no small or superficial task, but the rewards last a lifetime."

Although O'Donnell kept constant and extensive notes and videos of her works and classes, along with a description of movements, their counts, and floor patterns, the notebook stick figures remain her personal notation and memory aid and are not translatable.

One notebook is dated 1985, another 1986, and they were probably used to document rehearsals of *Powers of Ten* (1984) and *Holiday for Four* (1984). Earlier works do not appear to be recorded in notebooks. The name Bartok is mentioned as a clue that the description refers to a rehearsal of *Footfalls Echo in Memory* (1957). *Pursuit of Happiness* (1977) is also mentioned in her notes. In 1985 and 1986, her group performed at colleges and the New York City Ninety-second Street "Y," and the rehearsals probably were in preparation for those events, as well as for her video documentation project.

The notes include the month and day of the rehearsals as well as the name of the individual dancer performing the movement (Lisa, Lynn, Alan, Dale, and others) and May's charming stick figures. Here and there the name of a movement is given, such as "barrel roll" or "Shiva turn," without further description.

As a record, the notebooks remain personal and finally unfathomable, but they give us a glimpse into her diligent process.

Fifteen

Technique for Sit-Down Dancers

In 1994, Barbara and Sabatino Verlezza had completed almost fifteen years of their professional dance careers in New York City as professional dancers in the May O'Donnell Dance Company and in their own company, Verlezza Dance. In addition, they had taught at Adelphi University, Marymount Manhattan College, and Dowling College. In 1992, Verlezza Dance was invited to perform at a festival at the Theater of the Riverside Church. At that festival, they saw disabled Mary Verdi-Fletcher perform in a wheelchair. The meeting inspired mutual respect and interest in collaborating, sharing information, and exploring the possibilities of integrating dance between stand-up and sit-down dancers. Two years later, Sabatino was offered, by Verdi-Fletcher, the directorship to build a full-time company, educational programs, and a touring schedule for the already existing Dancing Wheels in Cleveland, Ohio.

The Dancing Wheels technique is based on the teachings of O'Donnell, who gave the Verlezzas permission to "translate" her vocabulary for sit-down dancers. In their wheelchair training, which is extensive and inventive, the Verlezzas use the contraction-and-release principle, spirals, and other movements that have proven a strengthening technique for those with injury or paralysis by increasing their range of motion and balance and thereby giving dimension to their body expression and enriching their performance quality. The technique pays strict attention to the rhythm, shape, balance, and dynamic of the movements.

As an example, if a stand-up dancer is in a one-leg balance with arms extended overhead with a focus upward, the sit-down dancer "translates" the position by lifting the front end of the wheelchair, balancing on the back two wheels, and, depending upon the technical prowess of the dancer, extending one arm above or, with an exceptional technician, extending both arms, even momentarily.

In another example, in going across the floor, a stand-up dancer may jump 4 times in First Position, followed by a step and brush leap 2 times, with arms in second arabesque, landing and repeating the combination. The sit-down dancer can tap the front wheels on the floor 4 times and push forward with both hands, arms ending in second arabesque position, and repeat the combination.

Barbara and Sabatino Verlezza have been guest teachers of the "translated" O'Donnell technique throughout the United States and in Europe. The company has performed as many as three hundred performances yearly and has appeared frequently on television

In celebration of May's birthday in 1996, the Verlezzas staged excerpts from O'Donnell's *Pursuit of Happiness* and *Dance Energies* using some sit-down Dancing Wheels dancers and some stand-up dancers in performance.

Sixteen Lifetime Achievement Award

"One, two, three," and Pedro, May's cat, jumps on cue onto her lap. May received visitors from the Martha Hill Lifetime Achievement Award, who informed her that she was the recipient of the 2002 honor, along with Doris Hering, dance reviewer.

December 1, 2002

"I don't know about honoring me, when it should all be about Martha Hill."

It *is* about Martha Hill.

"I don't know if I want to go." May has seldom been out of the house since Ray's death in 1997.

What would Ray want you to do?

"I guess he would want me to show up for Martha Hill. We used to visit her every Saturday at her open house. We weren't very social, but we did manage to go there regularly, and we enjoyed her guests. They were dance people."

May looks out from her living room window. She thinks about going to the reception. The weather is mild, but the trees are bare. Christmas lights blink around the windows of her street.

"I suppose it would be a good time to visit with old friends and students and dancers."

Yes, it would.

"What shall I wear?" Pause. "My long black skirt, definitely."

Definitely.

"I'll have to think about the rest."

Right.

A photographer has come from the *New York Times* to take her picture for an article by Jennifer Dunning on the award. May sits in a high-backed chair near a living room window. Pedro will have none of it. He heads for the floor of the dining room radiator despite May's coaxing him to be in the photo.

The photographer is skilled in seeing the best points in subjects who are aging. He likes May's long fingers, and she, becoming the performer once more, rises to the occasion with charm and places herself to best advantage. She and the photographer get along easily. The photo and article appear in the *Times* the day of the award.

December 2, 2002

May's gray hair has been freshly washed and combed straight below her ears. She has decided to wear a green East Indian tunic and jade beads with her black skirt.

55. May outside the Joyce Theater, 1983, with May O'Donnell Dance Company on the marquee.

56. May O'Donnell, 1980s.

"I'm a Green after all," she points out.

You are.

She smiles into a mirror. "If I had known I was going to live this long," she chuckles, her sense of humor still intact, "I would have had my two front teeth replaced!"

You still can. We laugh.

"What shall I say? There's a two-minute limit."

Let's rehearse.

5:30 p.m. It's time to go to the award presentation and dinner at a Chinese restaurant. May has choreographed her descent from her front brownstone steps with the help of two tall, handsome neighbors. She is held aloft in her wheelchair and bundled into a car. Roberto Garcia of the O'Donnell-Green Foundation, who has made all the arrangements for May's care, assists.

On the way past Tompkins Park, she remarks on all the new and old shops since her last trip outdoors. It is a mild night with no hint of the winter to come. The dark blue sky is a perfect backdrop for the twinkling holiday lights on the trees along Park Avenue. The dome of the Chrysler Building shines like the headdress of an Indonesian dancer.

The moment May enters the reception area, she is surrounded by friends, all kissing, laughing, excited to see her, and wanting to be remembered. A video of one of May's works plays on a screen. A long table has a center place for the master of ceremonies, Carmen de Lavallade, Norman Walker, writers Jack Anderson and George Dorris, Doris Hering, and Genevieve Oswald (first curator of the Dance Collection of the New York Public Library). Irwin Denis, president of the board of directors of the Martha Hill Dance Fund, welcomes the 180 guests. One of the speakers makes a long speech, and May naughtily whispers, "I thought we were limited to two minutes!"

Never mind.

Norman Walker, her former student and company member, and now director of the dance department at the University of Illinois, gives a brief biography of May's training, career, and companies. Then he adds: "I remember a different May O'Donnell: a woman of heroic stature, mythic beauty, and uncompromising standards of artistry and discipline. She instilled in me a work ethic that I try to pass on to my students. She allowed me to work under her guidance, thereby teaching me to find myself as a person and as an artist. She made it possible for so many of us to live our lives in dance and to trust that life as practical and sacred. She was our example, our guide, and we cherish the memory of our time with her."

May beams at the applause for her as Carmen de Lavallade presents her with the 2002 Lifetime Achievement Award certificate as dancer and inspired master teacher.

Although May has several rehearsed versions of an acceptance speech ready, she decides to forget about them and speak from the moment and from her heart.

"I'm so happy to be here tonight," she begins, "and I love you all! You are my dance world, my dance extension. I'm not supposed to talk too long [*laughter from the audience*]. I can't explain what a great experience it is if you know how to live in dance. It's more than a surface show. It goes down to your soul and comes out as something forever. There have been some wonderful things happening in our century, and there will be even more to come. We must always remember our dear Martha Hill."

Suddenly May changes the pace and direction of her speech.

"I wish all of you would do a certain step. Lift your right foot!" The audience, some sitting, some standing, obediently raise a right foot with delight and in surprise. May is once again the choreographer.

"We have to have some fun," she offers by way of explanation. But she doesn't tell her audience, now roaring with laughter, to return the right foot to the floor!

"We mustn't forget Martha Hill. She was the one who opened the doors to the dance that we are in today, to everyone, not in just one place or one time. We've been lucky. Thank you."

"How did I do?" she whispers.

You were great.

Prolonged stand-up applause follows. A bronze statuette of a dancer in a swirling skirt, created by Hortense Lieberthal Zera, is placed before her to be kept for one year until the next awardee receives it in 2003. Again, May the performer hides her surprise and embraces the statuette. "You see how beautiful dance can be, and how wonderful to be a part of it."

The rest of the evening, May is surrounded by people photographing her, hugging and kissing her and each other in joyful reunions.

May rides home behind bouquets of flowers. For days afterward, she is visited by family members who have come from out-of-town, dancers, and local friends who have come to honor her.

Documented Choreography of May O'Donnell

1937	*Of Pioneer Women*	Ray Green
1939	*Three Inventories of Casey Jones* (with José Limón)	Ray Green
	Jig for a Concert (with José Limón)	Ray Green
	Hymn Tunes (with José Limón)	Ray Green
	Dance Set (with José Limón)	Ray Green
1941	*On American Themes* (with José Limón)	Ray Green
	War Lyrics (with Limón) (retitled *Three Women*)	Ray Green
	This Story Is Legend (with José Limón)	Ray Green
	Theme and Variations (with José Limón)	Ray Green
1943	*Suspension* (first version)	Ray Green
1945	*Theme and Variations* (with Erick Hawkins)	Ray Green
	Running Set (with Erick Hawkins)	Ray Green
1946	*Our Rivers, Our Cradles* (River Primeval, River of Wrath, River of Desolation, River Song)	Ray Green
1949	*Praeludium*	Ray Green
	Horizon Song	Ray Green
	Fanfare in Jig Time	Ray Green
	Celtic Ritual	Henry Cowell
	Fortress of Tragedy	Ray Green
	Forsaken Gardens	Ray Green
1950	*Magic Ceremony*	Henry Cowell
1951	*Ritual of Transition*	Edgard Varese

1952	*Spell of Silence*	Charles Ives
	Act of Renunciation	Charles Ruggles
	Dance Sonata #1	Charles Jones
	Queen's Obsession ('52, '59) (Macbeth theme)	Ray Green
1953	*Concertino*	Charles Jones
	Dance Sonata #2	Ray Green
1954	*Legendary Forest*	Eugene Hemmer
	Dance Concerto	Béla Bartok
	Incredible Adventure	Paul Bowles
1956	*Lilacs and Portals*	Carl Ruggles
	Illuminations	J. S. Bach
1957	*Inventions*	Ray Green
	Footfalls Echo in Memory	Béla Bartok
	Sonata in D	Ray Green
	Pelléas and Melisande	Carl Ruggles
1958	*The Threshold* (Second Seven)	Léon Kirschner
	Drift (Second Seven)	Anton Webern
	Dance Sonata #2	Ray Green
1959	*Dance Energies*	Ray Green
	The Haunted (Electra theme)	Ray Green
1961	*Sunday Sing Symphony*	Ray Green
	Dance Contrasts with Three Dancers	David Van Vactor
1962	*Dance Scherzos*	Ray Green
1977	*Pursuit of Happiness*	Ray Green
1978	*Vibrations*	Ray Green
1979	*In Praise of Chopin*	Chopin
	Sonata in B-flat	Ray Green
1980	*Homage to Shiva*	Traditional

1981	*Fanfare and Devotion*	Ray Green
	Three Nocturnes and a Quartet	Chopin
1982	*Echoes of a Lost Land*	Ray Green
1983	*There Is a Time for Innocence*	Ray Green
1984	*Powers of Ten*	Ray Green
	Holiday for Four	Ray Green
1987	*Polka Sonatina*	Ray Green
1988	*Etudes and Scherzos*	Ray Green
1993	*Praeludium* (revised)	Ray Green

O'Donnell created countless undocumented works for her workshop classes and at the High School for the Performing Arts.

Available Choreography on Video (Including Copyright)

Music is available on tape or as a score. All were produced in 1991.

Pursuit of Happiness (1977; original version with four sections as solo)

Pursuit of Happiness (1989 version with four sections as trio)

Drift (1958)

Holiday for Four and Friends (1984)

Three Nocturnes and a Quartet (1981)

Dance Energies (1959)

Dance Concerto (1954)

Vibrations (1978)

Homage to Shiva (1980)

All music is by Ray Green except for *Three Nocturnes* (Chopin) and *Dance Concerto* by Bartok. Differences in dates of composition and date of choreography indicate composition was created before or at the time of the choreographic premiere. Differences may also be due to revisions. The above list, however, is based on saved programs. Information is available for restaging the works from the O'Donnell-Green Music and Dance Foundation, 263 E 7th Street, New York, N.Y., 10009.

Documented Works of Ray Green

According to pianist Emily White: "The powerful voice of Ray Green (1908–1997) was felt throughout the twentieth century in the worlds of American music composition, music therapy, modern dance, choral direction, pedagogy, and music publishing. In addition to promoting American music through the American Music Center (1948–61) and the American Music Commissioning Series and founding his own publishing company, American Music Edition, Green strove to devise a harmonic system that was far removed from the European tradition and an open, fresh sound that would appeal immediately to listeners from all walks of life. Green incorporated elements of jazz, blues, American shape-note hymnody, American folk music, Asian music, microtonality, music for dance, and electronic music. His music has been played in concert with orchestra and in solo throughout the United States and Europe. Green felt that his music would reach more people if it was not too cerebral; he abhorred the highbrow and constantly devised vernacular tricks to remind his audience that they should never fall for affected or convoluted sounds."

The collaboration between May O'Donnell as choreographer and Ray Green as composer is unprecedented, except for seven works created by Louis Horst for Martha Graham. The O'Donnell-Green collaboration produced more than forty works. Some titles are listed more than once because of revisions for a different group of instruments or because they were composed in part at one date and completed, expanded, or published at another time. Often the work, when it was used with choreography, was adapted and revised to suit the needs of the choreographer.

Green also published a number of books on music forms as teaching tools.

1927   *Four Preludes for Piano Solo; Quartet; Prelude in F-Sharp Minor; Andante Energico; Song for Tenor*

1928   *Riogoros for Violin and Piano; Declamation for Viola and Piano; Prelude; Seven Eight Time; Andante for Viola and Piano; Lento for Violin and Piano; Song for Baritone*

1929   *Suite Ironico; Lento; Allegro; Suite for Violin and Piano; Suite for Viola and Piano; Beautiful Women;* Music Notebook

1930   *Dances for Piano; Perronik; Song of Saul; Rondo Patetico; Five Finger Etude; Gypsy Pieces; Allegro for Violin and Piano*

1931   *Suite in the Form of Theme and Variations; Some Cadences for Piano; Contrapunctus; Four Preludes; A Mood; Theme; Break of Day; Hey, Nonny No!*

1932   *Set of Piano Pieces for a Man Puppet; Pieces for String Quartet; Structures and Proclamations; Song; Song of Saul; Upstream; To Lucasta; To You* (Whitman)

1933   *Sea Calm* (madrigal); *Sonatina; Five Epigramic Romances for String Quartet; String Quartet; Five-Part Canons in Five Movements; "An American Agon" Sonata; Sonatina; Sonata Brevis for Piano; Two Madrigals; Break of Day; Chivalric Love* (madrigal); *To the Moon; One Invention and Ten Fugues; Caution to Poets*

1934   The entire issue of *New Music Quarterly,* by Henry Cowell, was devoted to Green's piano and vocal music; *Festival Fugues; An American Toccata; Four Short Songs; "The Birds"; "I Loved My Friend"* (revised in 1970); *Upstream; Fifteen Preludes; Fugues and Inventions in Classic Style; Sonatina for Piano; Four Short Songs; Songs to Children's Poems; Some Pieces for String Quartet; Three Inventories on a Texas Tune*

1935   Revision of *"I Loved My Friend"; Overture, March, and Finale; Iphigenia in Taurus*

1936   *Holiday for Four; An American Bourée; Three Inventories of Casey Jones; Festival Fugues; An American Toccata; Pieces for Children:* Piece to Begin, March, Melody, Piece to End; *Early Gothic and Then On*

1937   *"Adam Lay i-Bowndyn"; Care Away, Away, Away; Hymn Set for Two Pianos; Early Gothic and Onward; Of Pioneer Women* (dance): (Westward the Women, Markers on the Trail, Jubilation for a Frontier); *Electra* (incidental music for Blanche Yurka); *Concertino for Piano and Orchestra; American Pastorale; Prelude and Fugue; Jig for a Concert; Songs to Children's Poems*

1938   *Plainsong* (Veni Sancte Spiritus); *Fanfare and Processional Dance* (for Martha Graham); *Walkaround* from *American Document* (Graham

dance); *Westron Wind; My Sister, She Works; "At the Feet O' Jesus";*
Beachcomber (blues for jazz dancer on Pantages Circuit, choreography by Roberta Jonay)

1939   *"Lullaby myn lyking"* (Christmas carol); *An American Bourée; Fanfare*
Opening (prelude to *What So Proudly We Hail* (dance); *Union Wives*
(satire); *Three Inventories of Casey Jones for Piano and Orchestra*
(dance); *Sunday Sing Symphony; Processional Dance for Symphonic*
Band; Holiday for Four (chamber quartet; *Theme; This Story Is Legend*
(dance); *Jig for a Concert* (dance); *Rondo Running Set* (dance)

1940   *What So Proudly We Hail* (Fanfare Opening, Cornerstone, Of Pioneer Women, Sarah Goes A-Courtin'); *Hymn Tunes* (dance) (Markers
on the Trail, Sweet Solitude, Sweet Song); *Our Rivers, Our Cradles*
(dance) (River Primeval, River of Wrath, River of Desolation, River
Song); *Dance Set* (dance), *Jig Time; Epilogue* (from cornerstone);
Theme and Variations; Songs to Children's Poems (additional); *Concer-*
tante for Viola

1941   *On American Themes* (dance, Curtain Riser); *This Story Is Legend;*
Three Women (War Lyrics); Three Inventories of Casey Jones; Theme for
"This Story Is Legend" (dance); *Preludes and Fugues; New Set; Concer-*
tante for Viola; Conversation with a Cloud; An American Rigaudon;
Theme and Variations (dance)

1942   *Hymn Tunes for Group*

1943   *Tombstones and Headstones* (for chorus and cantor with orchestra);
Suspension (dance)

1944   *Hymn Tunes for String Quartet; Jig Tune for Orchestra; Ballad for*
Americans (soldiers group)

1945   *Opus One; Short Symphony in A; Country Dance Symphony; Westron*
Wind; Theme and Variations; Running Set; Children's Songs

1946   *Concertante for Viola and Orchestra; Kentucky Mountain Running Set*
(for school bands); *Opus Two* (a symphony with episodes and a
finale); *Praeludium; Theme and Variations; New Set; Sunday Sing*
Symphony (for trio and orchestra); *Concerto for Piano and Orchestra;*
Westron Wind (for chorus and soloist); *Our Rivers, Our Cradles* (River
Primeval, River of Wrath, River of Desolation, River Song)

1947   *Passacaglia* on an original hymn tune; *Praeludium; Theme and Varia-*

tions (a passacaglia with eleven variations); *Rondo Running Set; New Set; Concertante; Children's Songs; Dance Set* (a Rigaudon, pastoral nocturne); new *American Bourée*

1948   *Jig Theme and Six Changes* (for band); *Short Sonata in F for Piano; Jig Theme and Three Changes for Strings and Piano*

1949   *Folksong Fantasies* (for trumpet and band); *Footsteps Echo in Memory* (supplants *Forsaken Garden* in 1978 and 1979); *Concluded Lives; Praeludium* (dance); *Horizon Song* (dance); *Fanfare in Jig Time* (dance); *Fortress of Tragedy* (dance)

1950   *Duo Concertante for Violin and Piano; Rhapsody for Harp and Orchestra; Three Choral Songs; Corpus Christi; Short Symphony in A;* Ray Green Piano Courses; *Dance Energies* (dance); *Fugues and Interludes*

1951   *Short Sonata in F;* Teaching Sonata Series; *Horizon Song* (dance)

1952   *The Queen's Obsession* (dance); *Sonata #1*

1953   *Dance Sonata for Two Pianos; Short Symphony in A;* Ray Green Piano Courses; *Two Sets of Etudes and Variations* (Hanon); *Dance Sonata* (dance)

1954   Revisions

1955   *Short Sonata in D for Piano; Twelve Inventions for Piano Solo*

1956   *Summer Sunset; Rhapsodic Interlude; Pieces for Children; Cowboy Sonatina; March Sonatina; Polka Sonatina; Song Sonatina; Square Dance Sonatina*

1957   *Short Sonata in D for Piano* (dance); *Footfalls Echo in Memory* (dance); *Dance Sonata #2* (dance); *Inventions* (dance)

1958   *Dance Energies* (dance); *Rhapsodic Interlude; Children's Songs; Summer Smoke; Western Sky; Dance Sonata #2* (dance)

1959   *Three Dance Energies; The Queen's Obsession* (revised); *The Haunted* (dance)

1960   *Hymn Tune Set for Two Pianos;* Ray Green Piano Books for Young Pianists, books A, B, C, and D; Piano Teacher Series; Sonatina Series; Teaching Sonata Series; *Children's Songs; Polka Sonatina #2, #3; Scotch Sonatina*

1961   *Children's Songs* (Ballerina Waltz, Happy Holiday, Offbeat Polka,

Olympic Star, Rag Doll Waltz, Raindrops, Rainy Day, Toymaker's Shop); *Sunday Sing Symphony* (dance)

1962   *Short Sonata in C for Piano Solo; Prelude Blues; American Sonatinas; Dance Scherzos* (dance)

1963–70   Sabbatical from composing

1970   Revision of *"I Loved My Friend"* (1935); revision of *Short Sonata in D; Prelude and Nocturne*

1973   New finale for *Dance Energies; Short Symphony in F*

1974   *Short Symphony in C; Short Sonata in D* (revision)

1975   *Forsaken Garden* (to Debussy)

1976   Revisions

1977   *Pursuit of Happiness* (dance, compilation of big band tunes

1978   *Prelude and Nocturne; Vibrations* (dance); *Sonata in D*

1979   *In Praise Of . . .; Short Symphony in C*

1980   *Short Sonata in B-flat* (dance); *Concerto for Piano and Orchestra III; Powers of Ten* (dance)

1981   *Fanfare and Devotion* (dance)

1983   *Summer Sunset; "There Is a Time . . ."* (dance); *Rhapsodic Interlude; Prelude Blues; Three Dance Energies; Songs to Children's Poems; Holiday for Four; Innocence* (dance)

1985   *Concerto in D for Piano and Orchestra; Twelve Sonatas for Piano*

1987   Completed version of *Sonata in B-flat; Sonata in F*

1988   *Sonata in B-flat; Dedications to Chopin, Debussy, and Stravinsky; Etude for Igor* (Stravinsky); *Etudes and Scherzos* (one of six)

1991   *Symphony in C* completed

1992   *Concerto in D* completed

1993   *Symphony in F; Praeludium; Theme and Variations; Short Sonata in B-flat #2*

1994   *Concerto in D; Kentucky Mountain Running Set for Band*

1995   *American Sonatinas for Symphony Orchestra*

Bibliography

Grove's Dictionary of Music and Musicians. New York: Macmillan, 1986.

Slonimsky, Nicholas, ed., Baker's Biographical Dictionary of Musicians. New York: Schirmer, 1978.

Vingon, John, ed., Dictionary of Contemporary Music. New York: E. P. Dutton, 1964.

Vise, Sidney, "Ray Green: His Life and Stylistic Elements of His Music from 1935–1962." Ph.D. diss., Conservatory of Music, University of Missouri, Kansas City. Published as a book by the American Music Edition, 1977.

Green's publishers were American Music Edition, Marks, G. Shirmer, Leeds, Arrow, Chappell, Ginn' Axelrod, and Mercury.

Marian Horosko attended the Russian Imperial Ballet School and the Cleveland Institute of Music, and performed in summer stock as a teenager. After graduating, she performed in the ballet at Radio City; in Broadway's *Oklahoma!* and two other Broadway shows; in Hollywood's *American in Paris, Royal Wedding,* and *Prince Who Was a Thief,* and she became soloist at the Metropolitan Opera and New York City Ballet.

Horosko taught at the High School for the Performing Arts and Fordham University. Producer of a longtime radio series on the arts, she also worked as associate producer at WCBS-TV and WNET and served twenty years as education editor at *Dance Magazine.*

She produced six seminars on dance (Weidman, Balanchine, Martha Graham, Alvin Ailey, Harkness Ballet, One Hundred Years of American Dance, and others) and has written five books on dance. She is listed in *Who's Who in America, Who's Who in the East, Oxford Dictionary of Dance.* Currently Horosko is a dance critic, lecturer, and New York correspondent for *Dancer* Magazine.